IT'S NOT

SUPPOSED

TO BE

THIS WAY

OTHER BOOKS AND DVD BIBLE STUDIES BY LYSA

Embraced (devotional)
Uninvited
Uninvited DVD and Study Guide
The Best Yes
The Best Yes DVD and Study Guide
Unglued
Unglued DVD and Participant's Guide
Becoming More Than a Good Bible Study Girl
*Becoming More Than a Good Bible Study
Girl* DVD and Participant's Guide
Made to Crave
Made to Crave DVD and Participant's Guide
What Happens When Women Say Yes to God

CHILDREN'S

It Will Be Okay
Win or Lose, I Love You!

IT'S NOT SUPPOSED TO BE THIS WAY

Finding Unexpected Strength When
Disappointments Leave You Shattered

STUDY GUIDE | SIX SESSIONS

LYSA TERKEURST

NELSON
BOOKS

An Imprint of Thomas Nelson

Published in Nashville, Tennessee, by Nelson Books, an imprint of Thomas Nelson. Nelson Books and Thomas Nelson are registered trademarks of HarperCollins Christian Publishing, Inc.

Thomas Nelson titles may be purchased in bulk for educational, business, fund-raising, or sales promotional use. For information, please e-mail SpecialMarkets@ThomasNelson.com.

Scripture quotations, unless otherwise noted, are taken from the Holy Bible, New International Version®, NIV®. Copyright © 1973, 1978, 1984, 2011 by Biblica, Inc.® Used by permission of Zondervan. All rights reserved worldwide. www.Zondervan .com. The "NIV" and "New International Version" are trademarks registered in the United States Patent and Trademark Office by Biblica, Inc.®

Scripture quotations marked AMP are from the Amplified® Bible. Copyright © 2015 by The Lockman Foundation. Used by permission. (www.Lockman.org)

Scripture quotations marked ESV are from the ESV® Bible (The Holy Bible, English Standard Version®). Copyright © 2001 by Crossway, a publishing ministry of Good News Publishers. Used by permission. All rights reserved.

Scripture quotations marked THE MESSAGE are from The Message. Copyright © by Eugene H. Peterson 1993, 1994, 1995, 1996, 2000, 2001, 2002. Used by permission of NavPress. All rights reserved. Represented by Tyndale House Publishers, Inc.

Scripture quotations marked NLT are from the Holy Bible, New Living Translation®. © 1996, 2004, 2007, 2013, 2015 by Tyndale House Foundation. Used by permission of Tyndale House Publishers, Inc., Carol Stream, Illinois 60188. All rights reserved.

Page design and layout: Crosslin Creative

ISBN 978-0-310-09434-0

First Printing September 2018 / Printed in the United States of America

CONTENTS

How to Use This Guide   7

Session 1: The Birthplace of Disappointment   11

Session 2: Living Between Two Gardens   43

Session 3: Problems Placed on Us and Problems Within Us   69

Session 4: The Four Steps of Restoration   97

Session 5: When the Enemy Comes Against Us   123

Session 6: Kingdom Minded, Eternally Focused   151

Endnotes   170

Scripture Index   171

About the Author   172

In their
hearts
humans plan
their course,
but the Lord
establishes
their steps.
(Proverbs 16:9)

HOW TO USE THIS GUIDE

GROUP SIZE

The *It's Not Supposed to Be This Way* video study is designed to be experienced in a group setting, such as a Bible study, Sunday school class, or any small group gathering. To ensure everyone has enough time to participate in discussions, it is recommended that large groups break up into smaller circles of four to six people each after the video is viewed.

MATERIALS NEEDED

Each participant should have her own copy of this study guide, as well as her own copy of the book *It's Not Supposed to Be This Way*. This study guide contains notes for video segments, directions for activities, discussion questions, and personal studies that will deepen learning between group sessions. This study guide also tells which chapters of the book should be read before each group session. You will dig deeper into the book in the personal studies between group sessions.

TIMING

The time notations—for example, 20 minutes—indicate the *actual* time of video segments and the *suggested* times for each activity or discussion.

Noting the suggested times **in bold with the section heading** will help you to complete each session within the time frame your group has available.

If your group meets for two hours, you will probably be able to cover all of the questions even in the longer sections. You will also have time for the optional activities. If your group meets for 90 minutes, you may need to omit the optional activities and decide how long you can spend on each of the other sections.

You may also opt to devote two meetings rather than one to each session. In addition to allowing discussions to be more spacious, this option has the added advantage of allowing time to discuss the personal studies and the chapters of the book. In the second meeting for each session, devote the time allotted for watching the video to discussing participants' insights and questions from their reading and personal study.

FACILITATION

Each group should appoint a facilitator who is responsible for starting the video and for keeping track of time during discussions and activities. Facilitators may also read questions aloud and monitor discussions, prompting participants to respond and ensuring that everyone has an opportunity to participate.

A brief leader's guide for each session is enclosed with the DVD of the video.

WEEK 1
SCHEDULE

BEFORE GROUP MEETING	Read Introduction and Chapters 1–2 *It's Not Supposed to Be This Way* Book
GROUP MEETING	View Video Session 1: The Birthplace of Disappointment. Group Discussion Pages 12–22
PERSONAL STUDY DAY 1	Pages 23–29
PERSONAL STUDY DAY 2	Pages 29–33
PERSONAL STUDY DAY 3	Pages 33–38
DAYS 4 & 5 BEFORE WEEK 2 GROUP MEETING	Read Chapters 3–4 *It's Not Supposed to Be This Way* Book Complete Any Unfinished Personal Study Activities

THE
BIRTHPLA
DISAPPO

ACE OF
INTMENT

Session 1

THE BIRTHPLACE OF
DISAPPOINTMENT

What would happen in our lives if we really lived in the absolute assurance of God's love in the midst of our disappointments?

Welcome! (2 minutes)

Welcome to Session 1 of *It's Not Supposed to Be This Way*. If this is your first time together as a group, take a moment to introduce yourselves to one another before watching the video. Then let's get started!

Opening Discussion (10 minutes)

Answer the following questions to prepare for this week's video teaching:

- How would you define disappointment?
- What was one sentence that resonated with you from the introduction or chapters 1–2 of the book?

VIDEO

The Birthplace of Disappointment (28 minutes)

LEADER:

Play the video segment for the Introduction, and then play the segment for Session 1.

Instruct your group to use the outline below to follow along or take additional notes on anything that stands out.

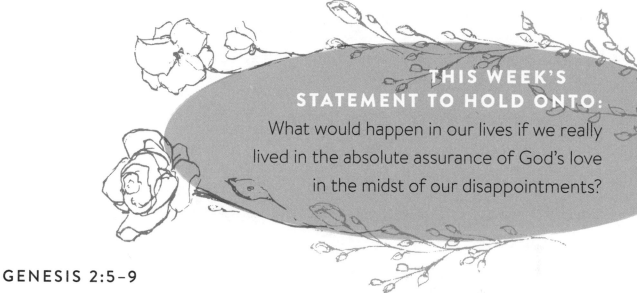

THIS WEEK'S STATEMENT TO HOLD ONTO: What would happen in our lives if we really lived in the absolute assurance of God's love in the midst of our disappointments?

GENESIS 2:5–9

v. 7: Then the LORD God formed a man

v. 9: . . . trees that were pleasing to the eye

GENESIS 2:15–18

v. 16: And the LORD God commanded the man, "You are free . . ."

v. 18: " . . . I will make a helper suitable for him."

GENESIS 2:23–25

v. 25: Adam and his wife were both naked, and they felt no shame.

GENESIS 3:1–9

"You must not" (Genesis 3:1) versus "You are free" (Genesis 2:16)

When God says "Do not = Do not hurt yourself" (Levi Lusko)

Eve assumed that she knew what a good God would do.

Created things cannot give what only the Creator can give.

You steer where you stare.

God could have been angry, but instead He asked two questions:

- "Where are you?"
- "Who told you that you were naked?"

Sin demands a sacrifice (Genesis 3:21).
In Genesis 3:22–23 (NIV), *banished* can be translated as "sent" in Hebrew (*shalach*).

Look at your disappointments through the lens of the great love of God. It will change how you see everything.

GROUP DISCUSSION

(45 minutes)

LEADER, READ EACH NUMBERED PROMPT TO THE GROUP.

1. What part of the teaching had the most impact on you? Take turns sharing with the group.

2. Lysa explained that the reason we face so many disappointments in life is that we are living between two gardens. There's a garden in Genesis 2–3 at the beginning of the Bible and a garden in Revelation 21–22 at the end of the Bible. Our hearts were created in the perfection of the garden of Eden, but we don't live there.

   Open your Bible to Genesis 2:8–25 and let's read aloud, changing readers every few verses.

   What were the wonderful features of this garden? List as many as you can.

3. What do these beautiful details reveal about God and His nature? List and discuss.

4. Why was the provision of water (v. 10) important? What does it reveal about God?

5. How would you describe the relationship between Adam and the woman (Eve) depicted in verses 18–25?

6. Sometimes we're trying to hold people accountable to a level of perfection in our relationships that's not realistic. Not that we permit or excuse behaviors in the abuse category, but what about those expectations we have of someone else who just isn't spiritually, emotionally, or relationally at the place where those expectations are realistic? How could understanding this help you in a current relationship that feels disappointing at times?

7. Is there a realistic option that could encourage growth in the relationship?

HAVE SOMEONE READ ALOUD:

The Hebrew for the words "suitable helper" in Genesis 2:18 doesn't imply a subordinate. The Holy Spirit is often described as our "helper" in the New Testament. And "suitable" here doesn't mean "good enough or just okay" but rather "perfect counterpart." A suitable helper is a needed counterpart, someone who fills a need that Adam can't manage on his own.

Jesus himself says in John 16:7–8, "Nevertheless, I tell you the truth: it is to your advantage that I go away, for if I do not go away, the Helper will not come to you. But if I go, I will send him to you" (ESV). Notice how the Spirit of God is described as our "Helper" in John 16:7. It's the Greek word *parakletos* and is translated as "helper," "intercessor," and "advocate." The essence of this word lends to the reality that the Spirit was called or summoned to aid and help the people of God. Therefore, the perfect, suitable helper was given to us by God the Father just as He gave Eve to Adam as a perfect counterpart.

8. What clarifying revelation do you have after reading this insight on the word *helper*?

9. Before sin entered the world, Adam and Eve had a close relationship with God and each other. Communication didn't feel complicated. Work was a pleasure, and Adam didn't have to toil among thorns and thistles in order to feed his family. Eve never felt the sting of comparison and struggles that seem to never end. Neither of them knew the bitter taste of sin or shame. How does this bring context to some of the situations in your life that make you say, "It's not supposed to be this way"?

10. Open your Bible to Genesis 3:1–9 and let's read aloud, changing readers every few verses, noticing the slippery slope of compromise.

11. Lysa highlighted the difference between "You must not" in Genesis 3:1 versus "You are free" in Genesis 2:16. When looking at God's protective commands, do you tend to view God as a "You must not" God or as a "You are free" God? How does that affect the way you relate to Him?

12. Eve assumed that even if they touched the fruit they would die. She added to God's rule which created assumptions. Sometimes we assume we know what God should do in circumstances as well. Give an example of a way you've done that before.

13. Remember, God wasn't removing Adam and Eve from the garden out of anger. He was actually protecting them. This was an act of mercy, not cruelty. If Adam and Eve had eaten from the tree of life, they would have lived forever in sin and would have been eternally separated from God. Write down how this example of His mercy, protection, and love could be playing out in your situation. Share your responses with the group.

OPTIONAL GROUP ACTIVITY AND DISCUSSION

Processing a Disappointment (25 minutes)

If your group meets for two hours, include this activity as part of your meeting. Allow 20 minutes total—5 minutes for the individual activity and 20 minutes for the group discussion.

Individual Activity (5 minutes)

Complete this activity on your own.

1. How would the way you walk through hard situations change if you processed all of your disappointments through the filter of knowing God is good and full of love and mercy?

2. Choose one word to describe this new perspective.

3. What area of your life would be most impacted by this new filtered perspective?

Group Discussion (20 minutes)

1. What is the most difficult aspect of processing life through the filter of God being good and full of mercy? What does this perspective require of us?

2. We know God asked Adam in the garden, "Where are you?" This is a profound question. Remember, Adam's physical location was not a mystery to God, but God was trying to call Adam out of hiding. The safest place to be exposed is in front of God Himself. One way for us to look at this in the context of our everyday lives would be: Where are you going or to what are you turning when you feel exposed or vulnerable? (*For example:* When you wake up in the morning, are you getting refreshed by God's Word or refreshing your feed on social media?)

3. Before the fall, it was common for Adam and Eve to walk with God in the garden. Picture them like little children hearing God's footsteps in the garden and running toward Him as if their Father had just walked in the door. But now that sin has entered in, they hear the Father's footsteps and are afraid. Sin always hinders our relationship with God. How does this play out in your life?

CLOSING ACTIVITY

(5 minutes)

1. Briefly review the video outline and any notes you took.

2. In the space below, write down the most significant thing you learned in this session—from the teaching, activities, or discussions.

WHAT I WANT TO *Remember* FROM THIS SESSION

Personal Prayer
(8 minutes)

Write a personal prayer here that reflects the area of this week's teaching you feel most in need of prayer.

CLOSING PRAYER

(2 minutes)

LEADER, READ THIS PRAYER ALOUD OVER THE GROUP:

Father God, it's hard to long for a perfection that will never exist on this side of eternity apart from our relationship with You. Disappointments are hard to navigate. So we offer to You our genuine feelings. You already know what they are better than we do. Thank You for loving us and standing with us in the mess of our disappointments. And we ask that You help us manage our feelings using Your truth, perspective, and holy discernment. We entrust this process of learning and growing to You. Give us the courage to make the changes we need to make and the grace to love others in their imperfections as well. In Jesus' name, amen.

Between-Sessions Personal Studies

LEADER, READ THESE INSTRUCTIONS TO THE GROUP BEFORE DISMISSAL:

Every session in the *It's Not Supposed to Be This Way Study Guide* includes five days of personal study to help you make meaningful connections between your life and what you're learning each week. In this first week, you'll work with the material in the introduction and chapters 1 and 2 of the book *It's Not Supposed to Be This Way*. You'll also have time to read chapters 3 and 4 of the book in preparation for your next group meeting.

PERSONAL STUDY

DAY 1: STUDY AND REFLECT

THE DISAPPOINTMENT CONTINUUM

Oftentimes we have a lot of feelings swirling around our disappointments, but we never process them. Let's do that now. We're not doing this to dwell on our disappointments, but rather to get to a better place as we process them.

1. There are various kinds of disappointment, from the annoyance of a friend canceling plans at the last minute to the devastating death of a loved one. Imagine a scale from 1 (minor) to 10 (major). What would you rate as a 10 on the scale of disappointments? What are some 8s and 9s? What are some 2s and 3s? Write down some examples below the continuum.

Minor
Disappointments

Major
Disappointments

1	2	3	4	5	6	7	8	9	10

2. How do you typically respond to a level 3 or 4 disappointment?

3. Have you ever suffered a level 8, 9, or 10 disappointment? If so, how did you respond to that initially? How has it affected you over time? How do you deal with it now?

To draw an analogy: a man's suffering is similar to the behavior of a gas. If a certain quantity of gas is pumped into an empty chamber, it will fill the chamber completely and evenly, no matter how big the chamber. Thus suffering completely fills the human soul and conscious mind, no matter whether the suffering is great or little. Therefore the "size" of human suffering is absolutely relative.

—Viktor E. Frankl, *Man's Search for Meaning*

4. Read aloud the above quotation by Viktor Frankl. How does this encourage you that your disappointments big or small are worth bringing before the Lord and being processed by truth?

5. Today you're going to reflect on the introduction of the book *It's Not Supposed to Be This Way*. If you haven't already read the introduction, please do so now.

The introduction begins by raising our awareness of how deeply most of us long for a life that feels "normal":

> There is a favorite story I like to tell myself. It's the one about how my life should turn out. Though it's riddled with missing everyday details, it's full of a general sense of okayness. No, actually more than okayness. It's the story where my toes can dig deeply into the sands of a glorious land called *normal*.
>
> *It's Not Supposed to Be This Way*, page xi

6. What are a few words that define the "good normal" you long for?

7. Pick a circumstance in your life that isn't what you thought it would be. What would your version of normal be around this circumstance?

> We feel very certain how things should turn out. But we live in the uncertainty of neither being able to predict nor control the outcome.
> Humans are very attached to outcomes. We say we trust God but behind the scenes we work our fingers to the bone and our emotions into a tangled

fray trying to control our outcomes. We praise God when our normal looks like what we thought it would. We question God when it doesn't. And walk away from Him when we have a sinking suspicion that God is the one who set fire to the hope that was holding us together.

Even the most grounded people can feel hijacked by the winds of unpredictable change. We feel weighed down by grief while at the same time unable to get our bearings as the weightless ashes of all we thought would be fly away.

It's Not Supposed to Be This Way, page xii

8. How have you tried to control the situation so it will turn out the way you think it should?

9. What would be your biggest challenge if your version of normal isn't the way things turn out?

10. Read the following verses from Romans, and then write a statement of release to God so you can have a marked moment where you entrust to God the outcome for this situation.

> [26]In the same way, the Spirit helps us in our weakness. We do not know what we ought to pray for, but the Spirit himself intercedes for us through wordless groans. [27]And he who searches our hearts knows the mind of the Spirit, because the Spirit intercedes for God's people in accordance with the will of God. (Romans 8:26–27)

Also read how Eugene Peterson phrases Romans 8:26–27 in *The Message* paraphrase:

[26]Meanwhile, the moment we get tired in the waiting, God's Spirit is right along-side helping us along. If we don't know how or what to pray, it doesn't matter. He does our praying in and for us, making prayer out of our wordless sighs, our aching groans. [27]He knows us far better than we know ourselves, knows our pregnant con-dition, and keeps us present before God. That's why we can be so sure that every detail in our lives of love for God is worked into something good.

Now write your statement of release:

We motivate ourselves to get through the bad of today by playing a mental movie of the good that will surely come tomorrow. And if not tomorrow, soon. Very soon.

And this good that comes will be such a glorious outcome that we will exhale all the anxiety and finally say, "Whew, I can honestly say it was worth it." Cue the redemption song and a small ticker tape parade.

The good outcome will look like we dreamed. It will come as fast as we hoped it would. And it will make all the wrongs right, right, right.

It's Not Supposed to Be This Way, pages xii–xiii

But if you are a human who has been doing the adult thing for more than twenty-four hours, you've probably come to the same stunning revelation as I have. We cannot control our outcomes. We cannot formulate how the prom-ises of God will actually take shape. And we will never be able to demand any of the healing from all the hurt to hurry up.

It's Not Supposed to Be This Way, page xiii

11. Sometimes God's promises are big instantaneous answers to prayer. Other times, they're progressive. We need to recognize the process of the promises. Name some evidence in your life right now that God's good promises are in process. If this is hard to see, list some things for which you're grateful.

12. Now, build on this. But in order to do so, you have to be actively looking for God's interaction and intervention in your life. Over the next twenty-four hours, challenge yourself to recognize evidence of God's faithfulness seven times and note each instance below. The more we look for God's faithfulness, the more we'll start to see it in a current situation that's hard.

-
-
-
-
-
-
-

> Though we can't predict or control or demand the outcome of our circumstances, we can know with great certainty we will be okay. Better than okay. Better than normal. We will be victorious because Jesus is victorious (1 Corinthians 15:57). And victorious people were never meant to settle for normal. . . .

> What if the victory is only in part how things turn out? What if a bigger part of being victorious is how well we live today?
>
> *It's Not Supposed to Be This Way*, page xiv

13. Open your Bible and read 1 Corinthians 15:55–58. What do you think it would look like to live victorious even in the midst of the hard situation you are currently facing?

14. What does it mean to you to be victorious regardless of how your circumstances turn out?

15. How does the promise that you will be victorious—better than okay—encourage you?

DAY 2: STUDY AND REFLECT

Today you're going to reflect on chapter 1 of the book *It's Not Supposed to Be This Way*. If you haven't already read chapter 1, please do so now.

The human heart was created in the context of the perfection of the garden of Eden. But we don't live there now.

This is why our instincts keep firing off the lie that perfection is possible. We have pictures of perfection etched into the very DNA of our souls.

We chase it. We angle our cameras trying to catch it. We take twenty shots in hopes of finding it. And then even our good photos have to be color corrected, filtered, and cropped.

We do our very best to make others think this posted picture is the real deal. But we all know the truth. We all see the charade. We all know the emperor is naked. But there we are, clapping on the sidelines, following along, playing the game. Trying to believe that maybe, just maybe, if we get close to something that looks like perfection it will help us snag a little of its shine for ourselves.

But we know even the shiniest of things is headed in the direction of becoming dull. New will always eventually become old. Followers unfollow. People who lift us up will let us down. The most tightly knit aspects of life snag, unravel, and disintegrate before our very eyes.

And so we are epically disappointed.

It's Not Supposed to Be This Way, pages 6–7

1. In what ways do you try to capture or project an image of perfection? How does the lie that perfection is possible show up in what you do?

2. How has the search for perfection disappointed you?

3. Have you ever looked at someone else's image of perfection posted online only to find out that their reality didn't match up with that perfection? For example, you've always admired how that friend's house looks on Instagram, but if you were to go over to her house, it isn't as it appears online. Or you look at someone else's marriage and hold it up as perfect, but then she confides in you how much they're really struggling. How do these misunderstandings and assumptions of other people's perfection taint your own life?

4. How do you think the enemy uses these pictures of perfection to compound our disappointment?

At Bible study next week, be prepared to share with the group some of the "less shiny" parts of your life that people might assume about you. These kinds of honest conversations will help everyone keep their own imperfections and disappointments in perspective.

We [either] don't feel permission to do so or we just don't know how to process our disappointments. Especially not in Bible study or Sunday church. Because everyone says, "Be grateful and positive, and let your faith boss your feelings around."

And I do believe we need to be grateful and positive and let our faith boss our feelings around. But I also think there's a dangerous aspect to staying quiet and pretending we don't get exhausted by our disappointments.

In the quiet, unexpressed, unwrestled-through disappointments, Satan is handcrafting his most damning weapons against us and those we love. It's his subtle seduction to get us alone with our thoughts so he can slip in whispers that will develop our disappointments into destructive choices.

If the enemy can isolate us, he can influence us.

And his favorite entry point of all is through our disappointments. The enemy comes in as a whisper, lingers like a gentle breeze, and builds like a storm you don't even see coming. But eventually his insatiable appetite to destroy will unleash the tornado of destruction he planned all along. He doesn't whisper to our disappointed places to coddle us. He wants to crush us.

And counselors everywhere are telling brokenhearted people sitting on tear-soaked couches that one of the reasons their relationships failed is because of conversations they needed to have but never did.

If we don't open up a way to process our disappointments, we'll be tempted to let Satan rewrite God's love story as a negative narrative, leaving us more than slightly suspicious of our Creator. Why would He create our hearts in the perfection of the garden of Eden knowing that, because of our eventual sin, we wouldn't live there?

It's Not Supposed to Be This Way, pages 7–8

5. "If the enemy can isolate us, he can influence us." How does this play out in your life?

6. To wrestle well means to acknowledge our feelings but move forward, letting our faith lead the way. What are some feelings that need to be balanced with the biblical truth you've learned this week?

7. What might moving forward in the midst of those feelings look like? How can you let your faith lead the way?

8. Read Psalm 88 in your Bible. It's a psalm of lament, a psalm of wrestling. Are you surprised that it doesn't end with everything resolved? How does this comfort you?

DAY 3: STUDY AND REFLECT

Today you're going to reflect on chapter 2 of the book *It's Not Supposed to Be This Way*. If you haven't already read chapter 2, please do so now.

> We live in a broken world where broken things happen. So it's not surprising that things get broken in our lives as well. But what about those times when things aren't just broken but shattered beyond repair? Shattered to the point of dust. At least when things are broken there's some hope you can glue the pieces back together. But what if there aren't even pieces to pick up in front of you? You can't glue dust.
>
> It's hard to hold dust. What was once something so very precious is now reduced to nothing but weightless powder even the slightest wind could carry away. We feel desperately hopeless. Dust begs us to believe the promises of God no longer apply to us. That the reach of God falls just short of where we are. And that the hope of God has been snuffed out by the consuming darkness all around us.

We want God to fix it all. Edit this story so it has a different ending. Repair this heartbreaking reality.

But what if fixing, editing, and repairing isn't at all what God has in mind for us in this shattering?

What if, this time, God desires to make something completely brand-new? Right now. On this side of eternity. No matter how shattered our circumstances may seem.

Dust is the exact ingredient God loves to use.

It's Not Supposed to Be This Way, pages 16–17

1. How does this revelation speak to you right now?

Read Genesis 3:1–7 again:

¹Now the serpent was more crafty than any of the wild animals the Lord God had made. He said to the woman, "Did God really say, 'You must not eat from any tree in the garden'?"

²The woman said to the serpent, "We may eat fruit from the trees in the garden, ³but God did say, 'You must not eat fruit from the tree that is in the middle of the garden, and you must not touch it, or you will die.'"

⁴"You will not certainly die," the serpent said to the woman. ⁵"For God knows that when you eat from it your eyes will be opened, and you will be like God, knowing good and evil."

⁶When the woman saw that the fruit of the tree was good for food and pleasing to the eye, and also desirable for gaining wisdom, she took some and ate it. She also gave some to her husband, who was with her, and he ate it. ⁷Then the eyes of both of them were opened, and they realized they were naked; so they sewed fig leaves together and made coverings for themselves.

2. What experience tempts you to doubt God?

3. What are you tempted to believe about Him that isn't true?

4. Read Genesis 2:9 and compare it to what you just read in Genesis 3:6. Do you see how all the trees in the garden were good for food and pleasing to the eye? Do you see how when Eve got fixated on the one thing that she thought would make her life better, she missed out on all the good things around her? How does this speak to a current situation you're in?

5. Read Genesis 3:15. This is known as the Protoevangelion (pronounced pro-toe-eon-gell-eon), the first good news, because it contains the first promise of the Savior recorded in the Bible:

> "And I will put enmity
>   between you and the woman,
> and between your offspring and hers;
> he will crush your head,
> and you will strike his heel."

Here, God speaks to the serpent in the garden. He promises that there will be perpetual enmity between Eve's offspring and the enemy. As the book of Genesis unfolds, it is revealed that the promised offspring of Eve will include the patriarch Abraham. God fulfills His covenant promise to Eve through Jesus, who comes from the genealogy (seed/line) of Abraham. Jesus is the one who has forever crushed Satan through His victory over sin and death (Galatians 3:16, 19, 29; Hebrews 2:14–18).

Why is it important for you to keep close to your heart the fact that even on the day when He was sending Adam and Eve out of the garden, God was already promising to send Jesus to rescue them and us?

6. Look at Genesis 2:25: "Adam and his wife were both naked, and they felt no shame." What were they designed for? What was their natural condition supposed to be prior to the fall?

- *They were innocent.* This innocence left Adam and Eve without shame and without any reason to hide from themselves or each other. Genesis 2 is a stark contrast to Genesis 3. When innocence was lost with sin, Adam and Eve were exposed physically, emotionally, and spiritually. Their first reaction was to cover up and hide.

  How do you relate to the tendency to cover up and hide?

- *They were without need.* Throughout Genesis 2 we see exactly how God handled every need for provision that Adam had (2:9, 19). God's provision did not stop at the fall but extended into the mess of sin. God provided clothing for Adam and Eve (3:21), and even this clothing had a cost: the death of animals. This was the first evidence of the blood that would need to be spilled to cover the cost of sin's consequences and restore and redeem all that was lost.

  What needs weigh on you often right now in your life? How have you taken those to the Lord and asked for help? How can you be more consistent with asking for His help?

- *They were confident.* Adam didn't doubt his purpose. He didn't doubt who was his Creator and King. Adam and Eve's confidence was based on knowing explicitly who they were based on who God was. The evidence of their confidence was their lack of humiliation at their nakedness. They felt no shame. In fact, this is the only place in Scripture where nakedness is not associated with some kind of humiliation.

  How do the effects of shame play out in your life?

- *They had perfect vision.* Adam and Eve could see in a perfect and unfiltered way. There was no confusion or disillusionment. They had no context of sin or evil, and so their eyes saw purely. The fall opened their eyes not only to the evil that now marked humanity but also to the good that they lost.

  How does confusion and disillusionment sometimes affect you?

7. Of these four aspects of the life you were designed for, which are you yearning for most in your current situation . . . innocence, needs, confidence or vision?

8. On the next page are some verses to show that no matter which of these aspects you're most missing, through a relationship with Jesus, God is providing these things for you today.

INNOCENCE

²²But now he has reconciled you by Christ's physical body through death to present you holy in his sight, without blemish and free from accusation—²³if you continue in your faith, established and firm, and do not move from the hope held out in the gospel. (Colossians 1:22–23)

NEEDS

And my God will supply every need of yours according to his riches in glory in Christ Jesus. (Philippians 4:19 ESV)

As for the rich in this present age, charge them not to be haughty, nor to set their hopes on the uncertainty of riches, but on God, who richly provides us with everything to enjoy. (1 Timothy 6:17 ESV)

CONFIDENCE

Is not your fear of God your confidence, and the integrity of your ways your hope? (Job 4:6 ESV)

For the LORD will be your confidence and will keep your foot from being caught. (Proverbs 3:26 ESV)

VISION

¹⁹For what can be known about God is plain to them, because God has shown it to them. ²⁰For his invisible attributes, namely, his eternal power and divine nature, have been clearly perceived, ever since the creation of the world, in the things that have been made. So they are without excuse. (Romans 1:19–20 ESV)

Write out which of these verses you want to commit to memory:

DAYS 4 & 5: REVIEW AND READ

Catch-up time! Go back and complete any parts of the study and reflection from previous days this week that you weren't able to finish. Review any revelations you've had and reflect on any growth or personal insights you have gained. Make note of them here.

Spend the next two days reading chapters 3 and 4 in *It's Not Supposed to Be This Way*. Use the space below to note any insights or questions you want to bring to the next group session.

WEEK 2
SCHEDULE

BEFORE GROUP MEETING	Read Chapters 3–4 *It's Not Supposed to Be This Way* Book
GROUP MEETING	View Video Session 2: Living Between Two Gardens Group Discussion Pages 44–54
PERSONAL STUDY DAY 1	Pages 55–57
PERSONAL STUDY DAY 2	Pages 57–62
PERSONAL STUDY DAY 3	Pages 62–65
DAYS 4 & 5 BEFORE WEEK 3 GROUP MEETING	Read Chapters 5–6 *It's Not Supposed to Be This Way* Book Complete Any Unfinished Personal Study Activities

LIVING B
TWO C

ETWEEN
GARDENS

Session 2

LIVING BETWEEN
TWO GARDENS

43

Jesus learned through His suffering an obedience that matured over time.

Welcome! (2 minutes)

Welcome to Session 2 of *It's Not Supposed to Be This Way*. A key part of getting to know God better is sharing your journey with others. Before watching the video, briefly share with one another any personal revelations you've had since the last session.

Opening Discussion
(15 minutes)

Answer the following questions to prepare for this week's video teaching:

- What insights did you discover in your personal study from last week or in chapters 1–4 of the *It's Not Supposed to Be This Way* book?
- Discuss some of the things you wrote down in your personal study time about your life that are "less shiny."

VIDEO

Living Between Two Gardens
(18:30 minutes)

LEADER:

Play the video segment for Session 2. Instruct your group to use the outline below to follow along or take additional notes on anything that stands out.

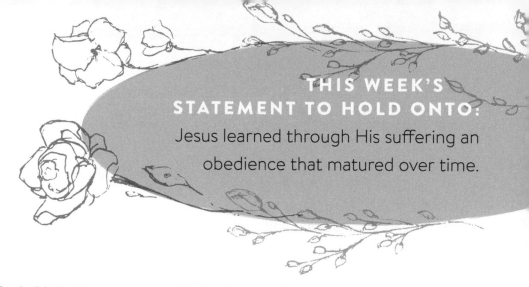

Revelation 21:3–6; 22:3: Eden is restored in the last two chapters of the Bible.

We live with anxiety from the first garden and with anticipation for the final garden.

Mark 14:32–36: The garden of Gethsemane is a picture of what it's like for us living between two gardens.

Jesus told the disciples to keep watch.

"Abba, Father, everything is possible for you. Take this cup from me." (Mark 14:36)

I can't start at my feelings and process my circumstances. I have to start with what I know is true: God is good.

HEBREWS 2:14–18

He [Jesus] had to come and experience the deep sorrow of this life between two gardens.

Since He knows what it's like to be human, we can know He understands what we're going through.

Fix your eyes on Jesus.

HEBREWS 5:7–10

Jesus learned obedience through what He suffered.

Genesis 14:17–24; Hebrews 7:1–17: Melchizedek was both king and priest.

Because Jesus knows the depth of what we suffer, we can trust everything He teaches.

GROUP DISCUSSION

(25 minutes)

LEADER, READ EACH NUMBERED PROMPT TO THE GROUP.

1. What part of the teaching had the most impact on you?

   Jesus cried also / struggles

   God said no to Jesus also

2. The last chapter of the Bible, Revelation 22, shows that our ultimate destiny is returning to the garden of Eden in the midst of a glorious city, the new Jerusalem. Revelation 21 says that the city will be built of gold and precious stones (echoing Genesis 2:12).

    Open your Bible to Revelation 22:1–5 and have someone read the verses aloud.

    • What will happen to the tree of life when Eden is restored? What do you think this signifies for us? *Can't imagine how it will be*

    Peace, Hope, eternity w/ him

3. You're returning to the garden of Eden, where "there will be no more death or mourning or crying or pain" (Revelation 21:4). How does knowing this help you?

    hope for the future

4. Open your Bible to Mark 14:32–36 and have someone read these verses aloud.

    • Why was Jesus' soul "overwhelmed with sorrow to the point of death" (v. 34)?

    • What could the disciples have learned if they had kept watch (v. 34) instead of falling asleep? Why is this so valuable?

    • Describe a time when you prayed for God to take away a situation or hard circumstance from your life.

- Why is Jesus' response, "Yet not what I will, but what you will," so important?

- What can keep us from wanting the Father's will?

- How does the story of Gethsemane illustrate what it's like to live between two gardens?

5. Turn to Hebrews 5:7–9 and have someone read aloud.

> [7]During the days of Jesus' life on earth, he offered up prayers and petitions with fervent cries and tears to the one who could save him from death, and he was heard because of his reverent submission. [8]Son though he was, he learned obedience from what he suffered [9]and, once made perfect, he became the source of eternal salvation for all who obey him.

- In the garden of Gethsemane, Jesus "was heard because of his reverent submission." And yet His Father didn't say yes to His prayer to be delivered from going to the cross. His Father allowed Him to endure all the suffering ahead of Him until His last breath. How does it affect you to know that the Father heard Jesus' prayer and said no?

- Why did the Father say no?

- When has the Father heard your prayer and said no?

- Jesus was able to be obedient to the cross because of what He learned from the sufferings He endured throughout His life. These sufferings weren't pointless. They prepared Him to trust God even in the midst of asking God to take away this cup . . . the pain of the cross. How does this provide perspective about the suffering you are currently experiencing? How does it help you to know it's not pointless, but the perfect preparation for a future way you'll need to trust God?

> No discipline seems pleasant at the time, but painful. Later on, however, it produces a harvest of righteousness and peace for those who have been trained by it. (Hebrews 12:11)

6. Turn to Hebrews 2:14–18 and have someone read these verses aloud.

- What was the reason Jesus had to be made like us, fully human in every way?

- How does knowing this change how you approach Him in your times of suffering?

- How have you been tempted to avoid the process of becoming mature through suffering? What have you been tempted to do instead?

GROUP ACTIVITY (20 minutes)

What we see from Jesus in the garden of Gethsemane is the holy exchange of His humanity for God's divinity. So now, let's make this same kind of holy exchange in our lives.

Following are some possible places we may need to make the holy exchange. Fill in the chart on the next page and discuss what these holy exchanges entail. Are they easy? Difficult? Why?

HOLY EXCHANGES

My Wants		for	God's Will
COMFORT	We want God to take away our pain.	→	God wants to develop our character. Romans 5:3–5 (read and summarize)
SELF-FOCUS	We want God to make our circumstances better for our own version of good.	→	God wants to take our healing to help others. 2 Corinthians 1:3–7 (read and summarize)
QUICK FIXES	We want to quickly get out of our situation.	→	God wants us to be positioned to produce long-term fruit in our situation. Galatians 5:22–23 (read and summarize)
IMMEDIATE ANSWERS	We want to know all the reasons and the step-by-step plan.	→	God wants us to know Him more and to develop deeper trust. Proverbs 3:5–6 (read and summarize)

OPTIONAL GROUP ACTIVITY AND DISCUSSION

Praying, Not Worrying (20 minutes)

If your group meets for two hours, include this activity as part of your meeting. Allow 20 minutes total—5 minutes for the individual activity, 15 minutes for the group discussion.

Individual Activity (5 minutes)

Complete this activity on your own.

Which one of these holy exchanges do you currently need to make in your life?

Group Discussion (15 minutes)

1. What will it cost you to make this exchange?

2. How will it help you?

CLOSING ACTIVITY

(5 minutes)

Complete this activity on your own.

1. Briefly review the video outline and any notes you took.

2. In the space below, write down the most significant thing you learned in this session—from the teaching, activities, or discussions.

WHAT I WANT TO *Remember* FROM THIS SESSION

Personal Prayer
(8 minutes)

Write a personal prayer here that reflects the area of this week's teaching you feel most in need of prayer.

CLOSING PRAYER

(2 minutes)

**LEADER, READ THIS PRAYER ALOUD OVER
THE GROUP BEFORE DISMISSAL:**

Jesus, we are awed by the fact that although You are eternal God and forever sinless, You took on human flesh and learned obedience and maturity through what You suffered. You experienced unimaginable disappointment, rejection, and physical pain. You carried the sins of all humanity in Your mind and body on the cross. You asked the Father to spare You from that suffering, and He heard You because you are His Beloved One, and yet He still allowed You to go to the cross. Please help us to walk in Your footsteps, seeking to do the Father's will, accepting the suffering that comes our way. We entrust our sufferings to You and we say, "Not our will but Yours be done." In Your name we pray, amen.

PERSONAL STUDY

DAY 1: STUDY AND REFLECT

Today you're going to reflect on chapter 3 of the book *It's Not Supposed to Be This Way*. If you haven't already read chapter 3, please do so now.

Chapter 3 goes back to the fact that disappointment causes pain. And we want to know what in the world to do with that pain. We can try to numb or avoid it, but, as Lysa says, "Feeling the pain is the first step toward healing the pain. The longer we avoid the feeling, the more we delay our healing. We can numb it, ignore it, or pretend it doesn't exist, but all those options lead to an eventual breakdown, not a breakthrough."

1. Which of your prayers feel as though they are currently going unanswered by God?

2. On a scale of 1 to 10, how would you rate the pain you're experiencing right now? Is it more like *let down* (2) or is it more like *desperate* (8) or *devastated* (10)?

Let Down   Devastated

| | | | | | | | | | |
| 1 | 2 | 3 | 4 | 5 | 6 | 7 | 8 | 9 | 10 |

> I saw myself desperately crying out to God. I saw no evidence that God was doing anything with my cries. I saw painful minutes turn into hours and then turn into days. I saw doctors scratching their heads. I saw tears in my mom's eyes. I saw fear in my family's eyes. I saw bewilderment in my friends' eyes.
>
> But I didn't see God doing anything about any of this.

And isn't that what deeply troubles us about this whole relationship thing we're encouraged to have with God? Doesn't a relationship mean you show up when needed?

Few things affect me more than being disappointed by those people who love me.

But being disappointed by the fact that God doesn't seem to be showing up during times of my greatest need?

That wrecks my soul.

It's not that I expect God to fix everything about my situation. But I do expect Him to do something.

It's Not Supposed to Be This Way, page 39

3. When have you felt that God wasn't showing up and doing something about your pain?

4. Has enough time passed that you can now see what God was doing? Or are you still mystified and wrecked by God's seeming absence? How is that affecting the way you relate to God?

5. "But in the end, it was the pain that God used to save my life." How does the outcome of Lysa's story help you deal with your own?

6. Being completely honest with yourself, are you more interested in the pain going away or in being made more like Christ?

7. Consider this statement: "God longs to help me." What gets in the way of you believing this? What helps you believe this?

DAY 2: STUDY AND REFLECT

Today you're going to reflect on chapter 4 of the book *It's Not Supposed to Be This Way.* If you haven't already read chapter 4, please do so now.

> If you get desperate enough you'll go all in with living slow for a while. You'll quiet down all the outside noise so God's voice can become the loudest voice in your life. Now, I realize, none of us can just quit life when life falls apart. But we can quit some things.
>
> I cut out almost all TV and social media.
>
> I cut out reading things online and chose to read God's Word more than ever before.
>
> I cut through the deafening silence of emptiness in my life by filling my home with praise music.
>
> I cut out as many extra activities as possible and spent more time outside with my kids and friends who came to visit.
>
> I cut out having lots of conversations with curious people and intentionally sought out pastoral counseling and friends with whom I knew I was safe to have deep conversations.

I cut out my speaking engagements and pouring myself out for others in this season so I could have time to be poured into.

And, I discovered something wonderful.

When you suffer, slow becomes necessary. Slow becomes good.

It's Not Supposed to Be This Way, pages 56–57

1. What could you intentionally take away in order to process your pain and hear God's voice?

2. Look at your answers to question 1 and consider some intentional exchanges you can make. Then write them in the chart on the next page.

INTENTIONAL EXCHANGES

Cut Out	and	Put Into Place/Action
Example: Cut out reading things online.	→	*Read more of God's Word.*
Example: Cut out having lots of conversations with curious people.	→	*Intentionally seek out pastoral counseling and friends with whom I know I am safe to have deep conversations.*
	→	
	→	
	→	
	→	
	→	

3. What fears do you have about cutting things out? Write them down.

4. How can you address those potential obstacles so that you really do carve out the things that keep you from hearing God's voice? Remember that you're only committing to a season, not forever.

What gives power to all that I fear others are thinking and accusing and saying isn't the people themselves. It isn't even the enemy. I'm the one who decides if their statements have power over me or not. It's me. And my desperate desire to stay covered up. I don't want to feel naked in any way. Even though I was technically in a bathing suit, I still felt so exposed. And I don't want to stand exposed, because I don't know how to do it and feel unashamed. . . .

If we were together right now, I'd turn to you, with tears of true understanding, and whisper, "Who told you that you were naked? Who told you that you are anything less than a most glorious creation of the Almighty God? Who spoke words over you and about you that stripped you bare and broke your heart?"

Whatever statement was spoken to you that came against the truth **must be called a lie!**

God's Word is the Truth. And His Truth says you are a holy and dearly loved child of your heavenly Father.

You are wonderfully made.

You are a treasure.

You are beautiful.

You are fully known by Him and lavishly loved by Him.

You are chosen.

You are special.

You are set apart.

> *No matter what you've done or what's been done to you, these words of God are true about you.*
>
> May we carefully choose what we remember and what we forget.
>
> *It's Not Supposed to Be This Way,* pages 60, 62, 64–65

5. What are some of the negative things you've heard from other people that made you feel labeled in some way? As a result, what are some lies you tell yourself that feed your insecurities?

6. One thing you can do is to rehearse the truth that refutes those voices. Write down the truths that refute the lies you wrote in question 5. Write them in positive words rather than negative ones ("I am special and of great value" rather than "I am not worthless"). Below are some truths from God's Word to help you. Look up the verse(s) listed for each one. Change "you are" to "I am" when writing your personalized truth statements.

   - You are wonderfully made. (Psalm 139:14)
   - You are a treasure. (1 John 3:1a)
   - You are beautiful. (1 Peter 3:3–4; Psalm 34:5; Romans 10:15)
   - You are fully known by Him and lavishly loved by Him. (John 10:14; Jeremiah 1:5a)
   - You are chosen. (2 Thessalonians 2:13; Colossians 3:12)
   - You are special. (Jeremiah 31:3; 1 Peter 2:9)
   - You are set apart. (Deuteronomy 14:2; Psalm 4:3)

7. Ask God to help you believe what is true about you and about Him. Tell Him any of the truths about yourself that you have trouble believing, and ask Him to get you to the point of embracing these truths. Write out a prayer for this below.

DAY 3: STUDY AND REFLECT

JESUS, YOUR HIGH PRIEST

Today, you're going to continue your Bible study in the book of Hebrews.

The book of Hebrews teaches us that Jesus is a fulfillment of the Old Testament sacrificial system. In the passages you're going to look at today, Hebrews also shows that Jesus is a greater high priest than the priests of the Jewish temple.

The Jewish priests were descended from Aaron, the brother of Moses. Jesus was not descended from Aaron. But Hebrews quotes Psalm 110 in speaking of Him as the great high priest "in the order of Melchizedek" (Hebrews 6:20; Psalm 110:4).

History lesson:

Melchizedek was the king of Salem (probably the same place now called Jerusalem) and simultaneously a priest of God. So when you see "Melchizedek," remember it means king and high priest at the same time. This was never allowed except in the order of Melchizedek, which we see fulfilled with Jesus. He is both king and high priest.

We first see Melchizedek in Genesis 14 and he is again referenced in Psalm 110.

¹⁷After Abram returned from defeating Kedorlaomer and the kings allied with him, the king of Sodom came out to meet him in the Valley of Shaveh (that is, the King's Valley). ¹⁸Then Melchizedek king of Salem brought out bread and wine. He was priest of God Most High, ¹⁹and he blessed Abram, saying,

"Blessed be Abram by God Most High,
    Creator of heaven and earth.

²⁰And praise be to God Most High,

> who delivered your enemies into your hand."

Then Abram gave him a tenth of everything. (Genesis 14:17–20)

In the passages above, Abram (Abraham) won a battle, and Melchizedek the king of Salem came to meet him. Melchizedek gave him bread and wine (a ritual meal) and a blessing in the name of "God Most High." In turn, Abraham gave Melchizedek a tenth of all he had won in the battle, thereby acknowledging him as a true priest and king. After that, Melchizedek disappears from the biblical story for centuries.

Then Psalm 110 has that quick and odd reference to a coming priest in the order of Melchizedek, a priest who would also be a king. He would have authority over the descendants of Abraham and would not be of the lineage of Aaron. The prophet Zechariah also points us to this very reality, that the promised Messiah would unify the roles of both priest and king (Zechariah 6:9–11).

The writer of the book of Hebrews, writing many centuries later, identifies Jesus as that priest-king:

> ¹This Melchizedek was king of Salem and priest of God Most High. He met Abraham returning from the defeat of the kings and blessed him, ²and Abraham gave him a tenth of everything. First, the name Melchizedek means "king of righteousness"; then also, "king of Salem" means "king of peace." ³Without father or mother, without genealogy, without beginning of days or end of life, resembling the Son of God, he remains a priest forever.
>
> ⁴Just think how great he was: Even the patriarch Abraham gave him a tenth of the plunder! (Hebrews 7:1–4)

Just as Melchizedek was a king, so Jesus is also King of Righteousness and King of Peace. Just as Melchizedek gave Abraham bread and wine to seal their relationship, so Jesus gave bread and wine to His followers as a representation of his ultimate sacrifice. By doing this, Jesus asked them to remember Him, and in our remembrance of Him we can be confident of our sealed relationship with Christ (Matthew 26:26–29). Just as Melchizedek was a priest who could lawfully offer sacrifice on behalf of others, so Jesus was the new and final high priest who offered Himself as the final blood sacrifice on behalf of all of us.

So what does all this have to do with you in your struggles with disappointment? It is an invitation to turn to Jesus as your high priest and king in the very midst of your struggle. Jesus is the one who finally and completely deals with all sin . . . the sins done against you and the sins you committed. He has forgiven you and enabled you to forgive.

And sending Jesus was not an afterthought on God's part. God planned it from the beginning.

Hebrews 2:17–18 says this about Jesus as our high priest:

> [17]For this reason he had to be made like them, fully human in every way, in order that he might become a merciful and faithful high priest in service to God, and that he might make atonement for the sins of the people. [18]Because he himself suffered when he was tempted, he is able to help those who are being tempted.

Because He Himself suffered when He was tempted, He is able to help you when you are tempted to hate, numb out, lash out, or commit any other sin connected with your disappointment. He is your merciful and faithful high priest. He shows His mercy in being willing to become a human being in every way while maintaining the full nature of His divinity (v. 17). He felt the depth of emotions and suffering you feel. Yet, he was without sin and faithful in doing the will of the Father, so he can lead you to be faithful in hard times as well (Hebrews 10:9; 13:12).

1. Write out your thoughts about Jesus being your merciful and faithful high priest. How will knowing that help you in the midst of what you are currently facing?

2. Why do you need Him to be merciful to you?

3. How does it help you to know that the Son of God became human like you in every way and still overcame the temptation of sin? What are you being tempted with in this season of your life? What help do you need from Jesus?

4. How has someone recently sinned against you?

5. Can you take a step toward forgiving that sin, knowing that Jesus freely forgave those who betrayed, abandoned, and crucified Him? Write down some thoughts about this.

6. How can the things that have been temptations and sufferings for you serve as a way for you to minister to others?

DAYS 4&5: REVIEW AND READ

Catch-up time! Go back and complete any parts of the study and reflection from pre-vious days this week that you weren't able to finish. Review any revelations or personal insights you have gained. Make note of them here.

Spend the next two days reading chapters 5 and 6 in *It's Not Supposed to Be This Way*. Use the space below to note any insights or questions you want to bring to the next group session.

WEEK 3
SCHEDULE

BEFORE GROUP MEETING	Read Chapters 5–6 *It's Not Supposed to Be This Way* Book
GROUP MEETING	View Video Session 3: Problems Placed on Us and Problems Within Us Group Discussion Pages 70–81
PERSONAL STUDY DAY 1	Pages 82–86
PERSONAL STUDY DAY 2	Pages 87–90
PERSONAL STUDY DAY 3	Pages 90–94
DAYS 4 & 5 BEFORE WEEK 4 GROUP MEETING	Read Chapters 7–8 *It's Not Supposed to Be This Way* Book Complete Any Unfinished Personal Study Activities

PROBLEMS
ON US
PROBLE
US

PLACED AND
S WITHIN

Session 3

PROBLEMS PLACED ON US AND PROBLEMS WITHIN US

God's promise fulfilled applies both to problems placed on us and problems within us.

Welcome! (2 minutes)

Welcome to Session 3 of *It's Not Supposed to Be This Way*. A key part of getting to know God better is sharing your journey with others. Before watching the video, briefly share with one another any personal revelations you've had since the last session.

Opening Discussion (15 minutes)

Answer the following questions to prepare for this week's video teaching:

- What insights did you discover in your personal study from last week or in chapters 5–6 of the book *It's Not Supposed to Be This Way*?
- How did the last session improve your daily life or your relationship with God?
- What is one thing you have learned about disappointment?

VIDEO

Problems Placed on Us and Problems Within Us
(18:30 minutes)

Play the video segment for Session 3. Instruct your group to use the outline below to follow along or take additional notes on anything that stands out.

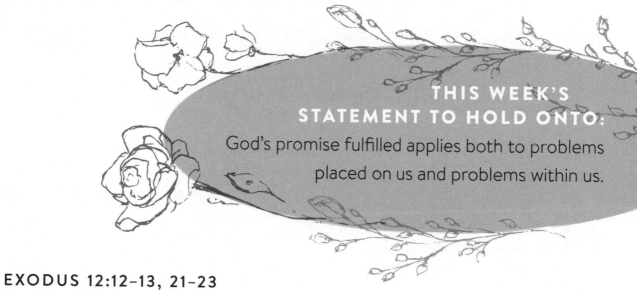

THIS WEEK'S STATEMENT TO HOLD ONTO:
God's promise fulfilled applies both to problems placed on us and problems within us.

EXODUS 12:12–13, 21–23

Truths about hyssop:

- It was used as the paintbrush to spread blood on the doorframes of the Israelites' houses so that the plague of death wouldn't strike them. [Example of a problem placed on them.]

- It was the purification ingredient in David's cry to be cleansed (Psalm 51:7). [Example of a problem within.]

- It was used to cleanse lepers (Leviticus 14:4).

- It was present when the promise was fulfilled by Jesus on the cross (John 19:28–30).

- Hyssop was one of the last things of creation that Jesus interacted with before He died.

God's promise fulfilled applies both to problems placed on us and problems within us. Both can be healed and fixed at the cross.

PSALM 69:21
Jesus didn't look to something to numb the pain.

GROUP DISCUSSION

(45 minutes)

LEADER, READ EACH NUMBERED PROMPT TO THE GROUP.

1. What part of the teaching had the most profound impact on you?

2. In the Bible hyssop is featured at moments dealing with both kinds of problems: problems placed on us and problems within us. We first see hyssop as the paintbrush in the Passover rite as God dealt with the problem of slavery that had been placed on the Israelites, from the sin of a cruel and fearful pharaoh (and even further back, the sin of Joseph's brothers).

Passover foreshadowed the cross. The firstborn of every family in Egypt was going to die because the pharaoh of Egypt refused to free the Israelite slaves. God told the Israelites to sacrifice lambs and to put the blood of the lambs on the doorframes of their houses. Any house that had the blood covering, God would pass over when He carried out this plague of death.

Have someone read Exodus 12:12–13, 21–23 aloud to the group:

> [12]"On that same night I will pass through Egypt and strike down every firstborn of both people and animals, and I will bring judgment on all the gods of Egypt. I am the LORD. [13]The blood will be a sign for you on the houses where you are, and when I see the blood, I will pass over you. No destructive plague will touch you when I strike Egypt." . . .

> [21]Then Moses summoned all the elders of Israel and said to them, "Go at once and select the animals for your families and slaughter the Passover lamb. [22]Take a bunch of **hyssop**, dip it into the blood in the basin and put some of the blood on the top and on both sides of the doorframe. None of you shall go out of the door of your house until morning. [23]When the LORD goes through the land to strike down the Egyptians, he will see the blood on the top and sides of the doorframe and will pass over that doorway, and he will not permit the destroyer to enter your houses and strike you down.

- Think about this image of dipping a stalk of hyssop into the lamb's blood and painting the doorframe with it so that the curse would pass by those in the house. How is this like what Jesus' blood sacrifice has done for you?

3. King David's problem was caused by his own sin, his decision to commit adultery with Bathsheba and then ordering her husband to be killed. After these terrible sins, David prayed:

> Cleanse me with hyssop, and I will be clean;
>> wash me, and I will be whiter than snow. (Psalm 51:7)

- God's forgiveness didn't mean that He shielded David from the natural consequences of his choices. David and Bathsheba's child died. As with David, there are still consequences of our choices even though we are forgiven. Do you ever struggle with this?

- What did God's cleansing provide for David?

Both the problems that are placed on us and those that come from within us find their ultimate solution at the cross. Jesus offers healing for both. Read John 19:28–30.

> [28]Later, knowing that everything had now been finished, and so that Scripture would be fulfilled, Jesus said, "I am thirsty." [29]A jar of wine vinegar was there, so they soaked a sponge in it, put the sponge on a stalk of the **hyssop** plant, and lifted it to Jesus' lips. [30]When he had received the drink, Jesus said, "It is finished." With that, he bowed his head and gave up his spirit.

- How does Jesus' death on the cross offer healing for problems that result from our sin?

- How does Jesus' death on the cross offer healing for problems placed on us and caused by someone else's sin? Can you make the choice today to let go of unforgiveness and bitterness?

It may be helpful for you to look again at what you learned in Session 2 from Hebrews 2:14–18:

> ¹⁴Since the children have flesh and blood, he too shared in their humanity so that by his death he might break the power of him who holds the power of death—that is, the devil—¹⁵and free those who all their lives were held in slavery by their fear of death. ¹⁶For surely it is not angels he helps, but Abraham's descendants. ¹⁷For this reason he had to be made like them, fully human in every way, in order that he might become a merciful and faithful high priest in service to God, and that he might make atonement for the sins of the people. ¹⁸Because he himself suffered when he was tempted, he is able to help those who are being tempted.

4. Because of the details the Bible gives us and the historical context of the Roman treatment of men being crucified, we know the immense suffering Jesus experienced leading up to and on the cross. The first-century church would have seen this cruelty firsthand. The Gospel of Matthew gives us this verse that details the last few moments of Jesus' life:

> About three in the afternoon Jesus cried out in a loud voice, *"Eli, Eli, lema sabachthani?"* (which means "My God, my God, why have you forsaken me?"). (Matthew 27:46)

Jesus' cry was a quotation of Psalm 22:1. This psalm as a whole is a picture of the suffering Jesus endured and the faith He held onto. But if we stay with this one "forsaken question" we can connect with the depth of the torment Jesus felt when He prayed "Thy will be done" at Gethsemane. He very much knew what he would soon experience during the crucifixion. So, when He cried out to God on the cross, this wasn't just because of the physical pain but also because of the emotional and spiritual pain of feeling utterly separated and abandoned by God.

- Jesus took on the weight of your sin so that you would never know what it feels like to be forsaken by God. Look up Deuteronomy 31:8 and write it out below. How does this give you hope?

5. Jesus had never before experienced the absence of His Father. In eternity they were united. Throughout His earthly life He had enjoyed an unbroken prayerful connection with His Father. But now, as He carried our sins, the chasm between a holy God and a sin-soaked man opened up. What do you imagine that was like for Jesus?

6. We often try to numb the pain of feeling distant from God. Jesus didn't do that. How does that play out in your life?

7. What is your takeaway from this hyssop teaching that runs through the biblical story?

OPTIONAL GROUP ACTIVITY AND DISCUSSION

(25 minutes)

Begin by reading Psalm 40:1–3 aloud. Then, read this excerpt from the book:

> And not only is His presence in the process, but there's also a purpose in the process.
>
> Longsuffering is long because you can't sprint through it. It's one step. And then another that might be more treacherous than all the previous steps. Getting to that solid rock from Psalm 40 might require a bit of a hike. Sometimes God lifts us up in an instant, and other times He wants to join us on a bit of a journey—a process through which we can gain a little more strength and grit and lung capacity for what He sees we'll need once we reach that rock at the top. There is a purpose to the process, and it's called preparation.
>
> If God thought we could handle the promise today, He'd lift us up today. But if we aren't standing on that firm rock, singing a glorious song, it's because He loves us too much to lift us up there right now. This process isn't a cruel way to keep you from the promise; it's the exact preparation you'll need to handle the promise.
>
> *It's Not Supposed to Be This Way*, pages 101–102

1. Based on what you just read, what do you now know about the purpose for a long season of disappointment?

2. How does knowing there's a purpose for the process help you?

3. Read the following verses and write down what they tell you about the purpose for your suffering or the promise that's ahead of you.

> And the God of all grace, who called you to his eternal glory in Christ, after you have suffered a little while, will himself restore you and make you strong, firm, and steadfast. (1 Peter 5:10)

> [9]For this reason, since the day we heard about you, we have not stopped praying for you. We continually ask God to fill you with the knowledge of his will through all the wisdom and understanding that the Spirit gives, [10]so that you may live a life worthy of the Lord and please him in every way: bearing fruit in every good work, growing in the knowledge of God, [11]being strengthened with all power according to his glorious might so that you may have great endurance and patience. (Colossians 1:9–11)

> [9]But he said to me, "My grace is sufficient for you, for my power is made perfect in weakness." Therefore I will boast all the more gladly about my weaknesses, so that Christ's power may rest on me. [10]That is why, for Christ's sake, I delight in

weaknesses, in insults, in hardships, in persecutions, in difficulties. For when I am weak, then I am strong. (2 Corinthians 12:9–10)

²Consider it pure joy, my brothers and sisters, whenever you face trials of many kinds, ³because you know that the testing of your faith produces perseverance. ⁴Let perseverance finish its work so that you may be mature and complete, not lacking anything. (James 1:2–4)

4. Which of these passages lifts your heart and changes your outlook the most right now, and why?

CLOSING ACTIVITY

(5 minutes)

Complete this activity on your own.

1. Briefly review the outline and any notes you took.

2. In the space on the next page, write down the most significant thing you learned in this session—from the teaching, activities, or discussions.

WHAT I WANT TO
Remember
FROM THIS SESSION

Personal Prayer
(8 minutes)

Write a prayer request here that reflects the area of this week's teaching you feel most in need of prayer.

CLOSING PRAYER

(2 minutes)

LEADER, READ THIS PRAYER ALOUD OVER THE GROUP BEFORE DISMISSAL:

Lord Jesus, it's hard to wrestle between how much You love us and some of the hard things You allow us to go through. And while we may never understand how all of this works together for a good that You see, we will intentionally look for the good You do reveal to us. And we declare our trust in You. A trust that doesn't have to know all the details to stand in the certainty of a faith in You. Thank You for the revelation about hyssop this week—this purple thread pulled throughout the Bible that breathes such confidence into our souls about Your intentionality and attention to detail. Let this spill over into our hearts and minds. You are also that intentional with our lives and You are aware of every detail that affects us. May our deepest desperations lead us to our greatest revelations about You. Lord, You are good even when circumstances are not. You are kind even when people are not. You are there for us even when all else fails. Your love carries us through and your compassion attends to our hurting hearts until healing is found. In Your holy name, amen.

PERSONAL STUDY

DAY 1: STUDY AND REFLECT

Today you're going to reflect on chapter 5 of the book *It's Not Supposed to Be This Way*. If you haven't already read chapter 5, please do so now.

> It was my moment to be the painter instead of the observer. It was my moment to face disappointment from the angle of an artist. . . . "Making art provides uncomfortably accurate feedback about the gap that inevitably exists between what you intended to do, and what you did."[1] And the gap never stays silent. It reverberates with commentary. Sadly, for too many of us it's a negative commentary. This is such a ploy of Satan. He loves to take a beautiful moment of life and fill it with a negative narrative about our failures that plays over and over until the voice of God is hushed. Satan perverts the reality that we are beloved children of God. He wants our thoughts to be tightly entangled in his thoughts.
>
> These are his thoughts. This is his script: *Not. Good. Enough.*
>
> *It's Not Supposed to Be This Way*, pages 74–75

1. Can you relate to hearing a voice that says, "Not. Good. Enough"? How are you learning to silence that negative voice so you can hear God's voice instead?

2. Lysa writes, "God wants us transformed, but Satan wants us paralyzed." With that distinction in mind, write down the words you think God and Satan are each trying to say to you in your current situation.

God's Voice

Satan's Voice

3. Lysa writes, "The enemy will do anything he can to prevent us from moving closer to God or connecting more deeply with other people." What are some of his strategies for keeping you from moving closer to God?

4. What are some of the enemy's strategies for keeping you from connecting more deeply with other people?

5. How can you connect more deeply with other people this week or this month?

6. How can you move closer to God today?

> This paralyzing lie is one of his favorite tactics to keep you disillusioned by disappointments. Walls go up, emotions run high, we get guarded, defensive, demotivated, and paralyzed by the endless ways we feel doomed to fail. This is when we quit. This is when we put the kids in front of the TV because nothing in the parenting books seems to be working. This is when we settle for the ease of Facebook instead of the more challenging work of digging into God's book of transformation. This is when we get a job to simply make money instead of pursuing our calling to make a difference. This is when we coast in our relationships rather than investing in true intimacy. This is when we put the paintbrush down and don't even try.
>
> *It's Not Supposed to Be This Way,* page 76

7. In what ways have you quit trying? Consider the examples of quitting that Lysa offers in the book excerpt above, and write down your own examples.

8. What is the paintbrush that God wants you to pick up and try?

Any time we feel not good enough we deny the powerful truth that we are a glorious work of God in progress.

We are imperfect because we are unfinished.

So, as unfinished creations, of course everything we touch will have imperfections. Everything we attempt will have imperfections. Everything we accomplish will have imperfections. And that's when it hit me: I expect a perfection in me and a perfection in others that not even God Himself expects. If God is patient with the process, why can't I be?

It's Not Supposed to Be This Way, page 77

9. How does the expectation of perfection affect you?

10. How does the thought that you are unfinished and therefore imperfect encourage you?

Disappointment begs us to be secretly disgusted with everything and everyone who has gaps, everything and everyone who also wrestles with the "not good enough" script. But what if, instead of being so epically disappointed with everyone, we saw in them the need for compassion?

It's Not Supposed to Be This Way, pages 77, 79

11. Who needs your compassion for their imperfections?

12. How can you extend compassion to them? Come up with at least one concrete way to show up with compassion in someone's life this week.

Remember, to show true compassion to other people you must also show compassion to yourself. What are some steps you can take to apply this to yourself?

"Praise be to the God and Father of our Lord Jesus Christ, the Father of compassion and the God of all comfort, who comforts us in all our troubles, so that we can comfort those in any trouble with the comfort we ourselves receive from God" (2 Corinthians 1:3–4).

When we show up with compassion for others, our own disappointments won't ring as hollow or sting with sorrow nearly as much.

It's Not Supposed to Be This Way, page 80

13. Offer to God a prayer of thanks for His comfort. If you aren't feeling His comfort right now, ask Him to help you see His compassion for you. Then ask Him how you can pass that comfort and compassion on to someone else.

DAY 2: STUDY AND REFLECT

In chapter 6 of *It's Not Supposed to Be This Way*, Lysa talked about the comfort she found in the story of Job. Let's study about his life a little bit more today.

Problems caused by forces outside us often feel unjust. Why does God allow them? Indeed, many people question whether a good God exists because they think a good and powerful God wouldn't allow the terrible things that happen to innocent people.

God rarely tells us why He allows any particular tragedy. Indeed, He may have many reasons, and we might not understand most of them. But He has given us the book of Job to show us some of the good He can bring from suffering.

Job begins the story as a "blameless" man who "feared God and shunned evil" (Job 1:1). He isn't perfect, but he deals with his faults in the way God has instructed, by offering sacrifices. God is so proud of him that He points him out to Satan as a person whom Satan has failed to corrupt. Satan responds by leveling a charge against both Job and God. Satan accuses that Job only loves God because of God's blessing.

> 9"Does Job fear God for nothing?" Satan replied. 10"Have you not put a hedge around him and his household and everything he has? You have blessed the work of his hands, so that his flocks and herds are spread throughout the land. 11But now stretch out your hand and strike everything he has, and he will surely curse you to your face." (Job 1:9–11)

1. God could ignore Satan's accusation, but He doesn't. Instead, He allows Satan to remove Job's wealth and even take his children to see the true nature of Job's heart. Does Job love God because of His blessings, or would he trust God even in the midst of great loss? How does this story relate to you personally?

Many read this story of Job and question God offering Job to be tested with such suffering. It's hard to reconcile a loving Father allowing this. But it's good to wrestle through the notion of a concept called retributional theology. Think of it as a transactional relationship with God that is directly tied to my behavior. If I do right, God will bless me. If I do wrong, God will curse me. However, the story of Job proves that this is not the way God operates! Instead, God uses the events in the life of Job to show us there's a greater purpose in everything we face that we may or may not ever know on this side of eternity. As a matter of fact, though the blessings in Job's life are restored, he never knows why all of this happened to him. Yet in the end he remains faithful.

But make no mistake, Job was not a robot. He was not superhuman. And, he very much struggled in the process.

2. Job 1:20–22 tells us Job's initial response to the horrible news of his loss:

> ²⁰At this, Job got up and tore his robe and shaved his head. Then he fell to the ground in worship ²¹and said:
>
>> "Naked I came from my mother's womb,
>>> and naked I will depart.
>> The LORD gave and the LORD has taken away;
>>> may the name of the LORD be praised."
>
> ²²In all this, Job did not sin by charging God with wrongdoing.

- What are your thoughts about a God who gives and takes away without explanation?

God next allows Satan to take away even Job's health, and Job's initial response is to defend God's right to do it. But then three friends of Job come to visit him. For a week they just sit with him in silence, sharing his grief. After that, though, they start giving him advice. They say there is one clear reason why Job is suffering: God is punishing him for some unconfessed sin. (And, because we just studied this, you now know this is called retributional theology.) His friends thought Job had to be at fault and needed to repent. They believed God rewards good people and punishes bad people, period.

Job responds by saying his affliction isn't his fault. He has done nothing to deserve it.

3. How do you respond to the wrong advice of Job's friends that when someone suffers they must have done something to deserve it? Have you ever blamed yourself (or someone else) for something that wasn't your fault (or their fault)?

As the weeks drag on with no relief, Job begins to question the goodness of a God who could allow such terrible and undeserved suffering. He says God is acting like his enemy:

> 23How many wrongs and sins have I committed?
>   Show me my offense and my sin.
> 24Why do you hide your face
>   and consider me your enemy? (Job 13:23–24)

4. How can we trust God's goodness even when He allows bad things to happen?

Job eventually demands that God show up and go on trial for allowing the righteous to suffer. And to Job's astonishment, God does speak to him out of a whirlwind. But instead of God being on trial, it is Job who has to answer God's questions. God shows him that he doesn't have anything close to the power or the wisdom needed to run the universe, so he would never understand the complexity of why God often allows the wicked to prosper and the righteous to suffer.

5. Even in the midst of all this hardship, God invites honest conversation with Job. And in the end, it deepened Job's relationship with God immensely. How can hard times

that force honest conversations with God deepen your relationship with Him as well?

Job obeys God by praying for his three friends, who have acted like enemies. Then God restores his health and blessings and gives him new sons and daughters who can't replace the ones lost but can at least give him solace.

God never explains to Job why He allowed him to suffer. He doesn't tell him about Satan's accusation. He doesn't tell him that He has used the situation to put a stop forever to the belief that all suffering is a result of actions by the one suffering. He doesn't point out that He has been refining Job. He doesn't tell him that millions of people are going to read about his story in a book and come to know God better by it. He may even have other reasons, but we don't know what they are. Ultimately, what helps Job is a right understanding of who God is. God remains good even when He allows hardships to happen.

But don't miss this crucial detail. God didn't just leave us to suffer alone.

God isn't just standing back watching us suffer. Through His Son Jesus, He willingly entered our world and experienced its miseries alongside us. And He wants to enter into our here-and-now sufferings and bear them alongside us as well.

6. What if God never tells you why He is allowing your disappointment? How does this story of Job personally help you?

DAY 3: PURPOSEFUL JOURNALING

Today, instead of doing a study, you're going to have a chance to process the hard things you are currently going through. You'll do this through journaling and prayer. Depending on how much room you think you'll need to write, feel free to answer the questions on these pages or in a separate journal.

1. List the top three circumstances in your life right now that feel too hard, heavy, confusing, or difficult.

2. Now that you've identified these three situations, spend some time journaling. The best way to get started in focused journaling is just to write. Keep writing and allow your heart to respond in full honesty with no hesitation. Journal a minimum of 10 minutes (more would be great), using the following prompts to process one of your situations:

    The hard situation I'm facing is _____.

    I feel (mad, depressed, panicked, numb, etc.) _____.

    This is affecting me by _____.

    I want _____.

cont.

I need _____.

However, after working through this study, I now know _____.

A truth from God's Word that is helping me in this situation is _____.

Now, you are going to transition in your journaling and use a practice of the ancient Israelites called lament: pouring out feelings of loss, pain, and the need to process with God. There are many examples of lament in the Psalms, the books of the prophets, and a whole book of the Bible devoted to it—the book of Lamentations. The practice of lament is not just pouring out our pain and sorrow but also intentionally calling to mind the hope we have in the Lord. A great example is found in Lamentations 3:19–22:

> [19] I remember my affliction and my wandering,
>   the bitterness and the gall.
> [20] I well remember them,
>   and my soul is downcast within me.
> [21] Yet this I call to mind
>   and therefore I have hope:
> [22] Because of the LORD's great love we are not consumed,
>   for his compassions never fail.

3. After reading Lamentations 3:19–22, in what ways do you relate to the author's lament?

4. Continue journaling, spending the next 15–20 minutes writing your own lament to God. Tell Him what the pain or frustration or hurt feels like and where it comes from. But also affirm what you know is true about God as you write. Pay special attention to the turn toward hope that the author of Lamentations makes and include this same kind of turn in your lament as well. For every sentence or few sentences of lament, write a truth of God's nature and His promises. Practice letting yourself feel the hard things while remembering God's goodness.

5. End your journaling time by writing a prayer asking God to help you live out His truth in your situation.

If you found this purposeful journaling to be helpful, you can repeat this activity for the other things you'd like to process with God.

DAYS 4&5: REVIEW AND READ

Catch-up time! Go back and complete any parts of the study and reflection from previous days this week that you weren't able to finish. Review any revelations or personal insights you have gained. Make note of them here.

Spend the next two days reading chapters 7 and 8 in *It's Not Supposed to Be This Way*. Use the space below to note any insights or questions you want to bring to the next group session.

WEEK 4 SCHEDULE

BEFORE GROUP MEETING	Read Chapters 7–8 *It's Not Supposed to Be This Way* Book
GROUP MEETING	View Video Session 4: The Four Steps of Restoration Group Discussion Pages 98–107
PERSONAL STUDY DAY 1	Pages 108–109
PERSONAL STUDY DAY 2	Pages 109–115
PERSONAL STUDY DAY 3	Pages 116–120
DAYS 4 & 5 BEFORE WEEK 5 GROUP MEETING	Read Chapters 9–10 *It's Not Supposed to Be This Way* Book Complete Any Unfinished Personal Study Activities

THE FOU
OF REST

R STEPS
ORATION

Session 4

THE FOUR STEPS
OF RESTORATION

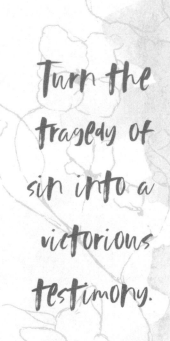

Turn the tragedy of sin into a victorious testimony.

Welcome! (2 minutes)

Welcome to Session 4 of *It's Not Supposed to Be This Way.* A key part of getting to know God better is sharing your journey with others. Before watching the video, briefly share with one another any personal revelations you've had since the last session.

Opening Discussion (15 minutes)

Answer the following questions to prepare for this week's video teaching:

- What insights did you discover in your personal study from last week or in chapters 7–8 of the book *It's Not Supposed to Be This Way?*
- How did the last session improve something about your life or your relationship with God?
- What is one thing you have learned about disappointment?

VIDEO

The Four Steps of Restoration (15:30 minutes)

Play the video segment for Session 4. Instruct your group to use the outline below to follow along or take additional notes on anything that stands out.

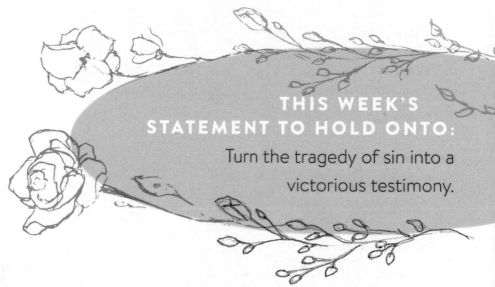

THIS WEEK'S STATEMENT TO HOLD ONTO:
Turn the tragedy of sin into a victorious testimony.

PSALM 51: written as a communal experience of confession within a community of faith

JAMES 5:16

From community we need accountability and empathy.

If the enemy can isolate us, he can influence us.

Sin never just affects the one who sins.

Four steps of restoration: confession, cleansing, creating, calling

Confession: Psalm 51:1–6

Cleansing: Psalm 51:7–9

Creation: Psalm 51:10–12

Calling: Psalm 51:13

GROUP DISCUSSION

(45 minutes)

LEADER, READ EACH NUMBERED PROMPT TO THE GROUP.

1. What part of the teaching had the most impact on you?

2. Turn in your Bible to Psalm 51. Have someone read verses 1–6, the passage on confession, aloud to the group.

   - Take a few minutes on your own to reflect on these questions: "What do I need to confess? Is it a sin I've committed? Or is it anger, bitterness, unforgiveness, or thoughts of retaliation for a sin someone committed against me?" Remember, God isn't looking to come down on you with blame and shame. He is looking to restore you. Search your heart and write some notes here. You won't have to share any of this with the group unless you choose to do so.

- Pausing to have time for confession with the Lord is an incredibly powerful practice. Discuss with the group what it was like for you to examine your heart.

- Do you have any habits that help you examine your life on a regular basis? If so, share them with the group.

- Look up and record James 5:16, keeping in mind the instruction that James is giving here is within the context of an intimate, mature group of believers.

SIDENOTE

Here are some important things to consider when discerning who within your community of faith could be trusted both to encourage you and hold you accountable in this area:

- A person who displays spiritual maturity in their life and has also been honest about their own brokenness.
- A person who really knows you and is invested in doing life with you.
- A person who you know has prayed more words for you than they have spoken to you or about you.
- A person who isn't covert about their own imperfections but is also eager to tell you about the biblical ways God is leading them.
- A person who you will allow to hold you accountable.

If you don't know anyone like this in your life, discuss ways with your group how to find a trusted person within your community of faith.

3. Have someone read verses 7–9, the passage on cleansing, aloud to the group. Though we briefly discussed this last week, let's consider cleansing after our personal confession.

- Why do you think cleansing is necessary when we have sinned?

- Discuss how we are we cleansed from sin.

4. Have someone read verses 10–12, the passage on creation, aloud to the group.

- In the Hebrew Bible, the "heart" refers to the core of a person. It involves feeling, thinking, and willing (decision making). What does it mean to have a pure heart? What is a steadfast spirit?

- How does God create a pure heart in us? In what way is it a one-time event? In what way is it a process? (See, for example, 2 Corinthians 5:17; Ephesians 4:22–24; Ezekiel 36:25–27.)

- Why is the creation of a new heart a crucial step placed after the confession and cleansing of our sin but before our calling?

5. Have someone read verses 13–15, the passage on calling, aloud to the group.

- From these verses, describe the calling available to us after confession, cleansing, and having a pure heart created in us.

• Is there a calling God is stirring in your heart based on all that we're learning?

David's season of confession, cleansing, and having a new heart created within him couldn't be skipped or rushed. Every step was necessary for this to eventually became a season of restoration and the fulfilling of his calling.

And, again, the same is true for us when we surrender to the Lord.

Notice that David wrote in verse 13 above, "Then I will" not "Now I will."

Sin breaks trust. Therefore, we can't expect God to entrust a calling to us before our full confession, cleansing, and having a new heart created in place of our broken heart. When trust has been shattered, it has to be rebuilt with believable behavior in our actions and reactions over time.

So, in time, David healed and rebuilt trust. Then he could teach others what he learned so others tempted with this same sin would turn back to God. When we go through a season like this, we can focus on learning about the compassionate nature of God and how to extend that compassion to others. In turn, it will be part of our calling. Just as David's pain turned into purpose, this can be true for us and the things we've done as well. Our longsuffering won't seem nearly as long or nearly as painful when we know God's perspective is to use it all for good.

It's Not Supposed to Be This Way, pages 138, 140

OPTIONAL ACTIVITY

(25 minutes)

If your group meets for two hours, include this activity as part of your meeting. You will need a package of molding clay. The purpose of this activity is to help us remember that God is making something beautiful out of dust, out of us.

1. Divide the clay into equal sized portions, one for each group member.

2. Then have each person take the clay and form it into something that reminds her of the "new" God needs to do in her life. (Examples: a flower, a heart, etc.) Consider the phases of confession, cleansing, creation, and calling as you form your clay.

3. Have a few women share what they formed their clay into and why.

4. After you're done sharing, have each member of the group place their clay shape into the box on the next page and trace its outline. Then, have them write some words in or around the outlined shape that summarize the process God is taking them through.

keep him on track
↑ clarity, leader

Morgan, Dakota, Michelle : field guy —
↑ wisdom   peace   wisdom to keep away lol

Aunt Becky, Mom-tricia, Jodie's family, Alison-healing
hip pain   ↑ passed away   car accid.

Randy - continued healing from Sx
Nathan : a new job - full time
Book back from editor - everything goes
        smoothly, little revision - perfect

- Boys good
- safe travels for Leah/Natalie travel
        sisters wedding, parents put everything
        aside for her day
- Natalie : math
- Becky lump - nothing (cyst)
- direction for Business - stable/steady
- contract - let her get it soon

= prayers for school staff Jr./High School
- focus for me

CLOSING ACTIVITY

What I Want to Remember (5 minutes)

Complete this activity on your own.

1. Briefly review the outline and any notes you took.

2. In the space below, write down the most significant thing you learned in this session—from the teaching, activities, or discussions.

WHAT I WANT TO
Remember
FROM THIS SESSION

Personal Prayer
(8 minutes)

Write a personal prayer here that reflects the area of this week's teaching you feel most in need of prayer: confession, cleansing, creation, calling.

CLOSING PRAYER

(2 minutes)

**LEADER, READ THIS PRAYER ALOUD OVER
THE GROUP BEFORE DISMISSAL:**

Dear Lord, You know our sins. You know the strategies we use to avoid our sin and our pain. You know them better than we do, and we invite You to make us fully aware of them. We confess these things to You, trusting in Your steadfast love and compassion. Please wash us clean. Create in us clean hearts, O God, and renew a steadfast spirit within us. Do not cast us away from Your presence or take Your Holy Spirit from us. Grant us a willing spirit. Stir up in us the joy of Your salvation. Thank You for the forgiveness that is available to us through the blood of Jesus. Lead us through Your healing process so that we can proclaim what You have done for us. We ask all of this through Your Son Jesus, amen.

PERSONAL STUDY

DAY 1: REFLECT AND PRAY

1. In this week's video Lysa briefly mentioned that when Nathan finally confronted David, David's response wasn't to numb his pain but to confess his sin. We talked a lot about confession as a group. Now, let's address how we sometimes would rather numb the pain than confess the sin surrounding it.

    Ask God to show you how this applies to you personally. Today's study is a bit shorter so you can take some time to really pray about this.

    Maybe you stay busy to keep from acknowledging what you're feeling, but when you get quiet, emotions start to bubble to the surface. What do you generally want to do then? Write down what you do when you want to numb your pain.

2. How does doing that numbing strategy affect you? How does it affect your time management, your waistline, your soul, your relationship with God, your relationship with others?

3. Are you able to just stop this habit? Or has it become automatic or controlling of you?

4. What is one step you can take to let go of this habit? For example, you could decide to pay more attention to times when you slip into this habit. You could also decide that when you notice yourself doing it, you will call out to the Lord, reach out to a friend, or seek the help of a Christian counselor. Write some scriptural prayers below asking for the Lord's help; use Psalm 86:1 and Psalm 91:2, 9.

DAY 2: STUDY AND REFLECT

Today you're going to reflect on chapter 7 of the book *It's Not Supposed to Be This Way*. If you haven't already read chapter 7, please do so now.

> God doesn't expect us to handle this. He wants us to hand this over to Him. He doesn't want us to rally more of our own strength. He wants us to rely solely on His strength.
>
> If we keep walking around, thinking that God won't give us more than we can handle, we set ourselves up to be suspicious of God. We know we are facing things that are too much for us. We are bombarded with burdens. We are weighed down with wondering. And we are all trying to make sense of things that don't make sense. Before we can move forward in a healthy way, we must first acknowledge the truth about our insufficiency.
>
> *It's Not Supposed to Be This Way*, pages 112–113

1. What is something you're facing right now that you know you need to hand over to the Lord?

The apostle Paul wrote:

> For we do not want you to be uninformed, brothers and sisters, about the troubles we experienced in the province of Asia. We were under great pressure, far beyond our ability to endure, so that we despaired of life itself. Indeed, we felt we had received the sentence of death. But this happened that we might not rely on ourselves but on God, who raises the dead. (2 Corinthians 1:8–9)

The original Greek word for "rely" here is *peithō* (*pee-tho*). The same Greek word is used two other times in 2 Corinthians (2:3; 10:7). The essence of this word is confidence. In verse 8, Paul lets us know the depth of what he faced. He felt as though his circumstances were a death sentence. This led him to recognize that his experiences were opportunities to come to terms with his great need for God. His near-death experiences created a "spiritual trauma" that changed him to the core. Rather than relying on himself, he became steadfast in his reliance and confidence in God.[2]

2. No matter what we're going through, we have the choice to have more confidence in God or less confidence in God. How can you make the choice in your situation to have more confidence in the Lord and learn to truly rely on His strength?

And the main thing I know? I know God is good. I didn't know the details of God's good plan, but I could make His goodness the starting place to renew my perspective.

So now let me tell the story of all these recent events using God's goodness as the central theme. Had things not blown up between Art and me last summer, I never would have hit the pause button on life to go get a mammogram. I would have waited. But because I had a mammogram at that exact time, the doctors caught a cancer that needed to be caught. And because they caught a cancer that needed to be caught, I had every fighting chance to beat this cancer.

You see, we're all living out a story, but then there's the story we tell ourselves. We just need to make sure what we're telling ourselves is the right story. And the right story is, yes, God will give us more than we can handle. But He always has eventual good in mind.

It's Not Supposed to Be This Way, page 114

3. Tell the story of your disappointment using God's goodness as the central theme. Take your time with this. Use Lysa's example as a model. Where is God's goodness threaded through? Intentionally look for evidences of God's goodness even in the midst of circumstances that aren't seemingly good at all. You may not yet know the good results God is going to bring out of your situation, but shift to seeing all things through the lens of being confident in His goodness.

A potsherd is a broken piece of pottery. . . . A broken potsherd can lie on the ground and be nothing more than a constant reminder of brokenness. It can also be used to continue to scrape us and hurt us even more when kept in our hands.

Or, when placed in our Master's hands, the Master Potter can be entrusted to take that potsherd, shatter it just right, and then use it in the remolding of me to make me stronger and even more beautiful.

When I understood this, I saw that in all my circumstances God was keeping me moldable while adding even more strength and beauty in the process. . . .

Take this, Lord, and shatter it just right, so I can be made stronger, more beautiful, and able to withstand fires as never before. I believe that You see things I cannot see. And You have eventual good in mind.

This perspective didn't take away my cancer. But it did take away the feeling I had to figure this out on my own. It took the weight of it all out of my hands and helped me release it to God.

It's Not Supposed to Be This Way, pages 116–117

4. What parts of this analogy can you embrace right now? Are there any parts you're resisting?

When we hit the place in our lives when we finally realize some things are truly more than we can handle, we will throw our hands up in surrender. And that surrender can happen in one of two ways.

We might surrender to the enemy, giving in to those feelings that this isn't fair, God isn't there, and God isn't good. Or, we can surrender to God. This kind of surrender isn't giving in; it's giving up! Giving up carrying the weight of all that's too much for us to our God, who not only can carry it but use it for good. When we know the truth about the amazing things God can do with the dust and the potsherds of life, we won't surrender to the negative lies of the enemy. Instead, we will lift our hands to the Potter.

It's Not Supposed to Be This Way, page 117

5. How does Lysa's explanation help you have a better view of surrender in your life circumstances?

> In the book of Jeremiah, we find that the children of Israel were going to be carried into captivity by Babylon for seventy years. Think about how long seventy years is. If we had to go to prison today for seventy years, for most of us that would mean we'd probably die in captivity. Seventy years feels impossibly long, incredibly unfair, and horribly hard. It would seem like a lifetime hardship without a lifeline of hope. Talk about longsuffering. Talk about feeling as if no good thing could ever come from this. Talk about needing God's perspective like never before! But here's what God told the people of Israel: "When seventy years are completed for Babylon, I will come to you and fulfill my good promise to bring you back to this place" (Jeremiah 29:10).
>
> This is the scene and the setting where we then get these glorious promises that I love to cling to:
>
>> For I know the plans I have for you . . . plans to prosper you and not to harm you, plans to give you hope and a future. Then you will call upon me and come and pray to me, and I will listen to you. You will seek me and find me when you seek me with all of your heart. I will be found by you. (Jeremiah 29:11–14)
>
> *It's Not Supposed to Be This Way*, pages 117, 119

6. What are some ways you can seek out hope in your period of longsuffering?

7. Name a few specific ways you can seek God with all of your heart in your situation.

> When we seek God, we see God. We don't see His physical form, but we see Him at work and can start to see more of what He sees. Trust grows. If our hearts are willing to trust Him, He will entrust to us more and more of His perspective. Matthew 5:8 teaches us, "blessed are the pure in heart, for they will see God." If we want to see Him in our circumstances and see His perspective, we must seek Him, His ways, and His Word. That's where we find His good plans and promises for hope and a future.
>
> *It's Not Supposed to Be This Way,* page 119

8. What is a perspective you've now gained for your life's circumstances by seeking God this way?

> And *this* is God's Truth:
>
> **I AM THE WAY AND THE TRUTH AND THE LIFE.**
>
> "I am the way and the truth and the life. No one comes to the Father except through me." (John 14:6)

I AM FOREVER FAITHFUL.

He is the Maker of heaven and earth,
the sea, and everything in them—
He remains faithful forever.
(Psalm 146:6)

I AM WITH YOU.

So do not fear, for I am with you;
do not be dismayed, for I am your God.
I will strengthen you and help you;
I will uphold you with my righteous right hand.
(Isaiah 41:10)

I AM HOLDING YOU.

Yet I am always with you;
you hold me by my right hand.
(Psalm 73:23)

I AM YOUR HIDING PLACE.

You are my hiding place;
you will protect me from trouble
and surround me with songs of deliverance.
(Psalm 32:7)

It's Not Supposed to Be This Way, pages 122–123

9. Choose one of these Bible verses and expand it into a prayer that relates to what you're dealing with right now.

DAY 3: STUDY AND REFLECT

Today you're going to reflect on the ideas raised in chapter 8 of the book *It's Not Supposed to Be This Way*. If you haven't already read chapter 8, please do so now.

> But here's the gift of my very messy moments like these. They make me aware that there are some things to address. It's when I stop pretending I'm fine when I'm really not fine. It's when I stop to address what's really holding me back from moving forward. And not just limp forward or crawl forward burdened down from what we've been through but to run forward with great freedom.
>
> *It's Not Supposed to Be This Way*, page 130

1. Do you tend to pretend you're fine when you're really not fine? If so, when have you done that recently?

2. What is holding you back from this? What would "running forward with freedom" look like for you?

> As he went along, he saw a man blind from birth. His disciples asked him, "Rabbi, who sinned, this man or his parents, that he was born blind?"
>
> "Neither this man nor his parents sinned," said Jesus, "but this happened so that the works of God might be displayed in him. As long as it is day, we must do the works of him who sent me. Night is coming, when no one can work. While I am in the world, I am the light of the world."

After saying this, he spit on the ground, made some mud with the saliva, and put it on the man's eyes. "Go," he told him, "wash in the pool of Siloam" [this word means "Sent"]. So the man went and washed and came home seeing. (John 9:1–7)

This man's blindness—his own form of hardship and longsuffering—wasn't because of choices he made or ones his parents made. This suffering was placed on him. But it was for a reason. He was handpicked to display the works of God. Through his story Jesus would shine the light of truth and hope for others' lives to not be so dark.

It's Not Supposed to Be This Way, pages 132–133

3. What feelings arise when you read "Neither this man nor his parents sinned"? Why is that important for you to hear?

4. In the group discussion for Session 4 we talked about how David's sin was indeed the cause of his problems. Right now, are you more identifying with David or with the blind man? Why?

5. What if you have been "handpicked to display the works of God"? What if through your story Jesus will "shine the light of truth and hope for others' lives not to be so dark"? Write down your thoughts about this.

Here's how Eugene Peterson paraphrased Hebrews 12:1–3:

> Do you see what this means—all these pioneers who blazed the way, all these veterans cheering us on? It means we'd better get on with it. Strip down, start running—and never quit! No extra spiritual fat, no parasitic sins. Keep your eyes on Jesus, who both began and finished this race we're in. Study how he did it. Because he never lost sight of where he was headed—that exhilarating finish in and with God—he could put up with anything along the way: Cross, shame, whatever. And now he's there, in the place of honor, right alongside God. When you find yourselves flagging in your faith, go over that story again, item by item, that long litany of hostility he plowed through. That will shoot adrenaline into your souls! (Hebrews 12:1–3 THE MESSAGE)

I love that Eugene gives us the secret of being a person who keeps going. Let's call it the secret of being steadfast. Jesus lived it so we could know it. Let's look again at one specific part of the passage: "Because he [Jesus] never lost sight of where he was headed . . . he could put up with anything along the way." That's why we must keep our eyes on Him and go over His story—the Bible—over and over again.

This is how we get through this life between two gardens. This is how we make sense of things that don't make sense. This is how we can believe God is good when life isn't good. This is how we can face hurt upon hurt, disappointment upon disappointment, longsuffering upon longsuffering, and still run our race with oxygen filling our lungs, peace filling our minds, and joy filling our hearts.

It's Not Supposed to Be This Way, pages 140–141

6. Jesus never lost sight of where He was headed. Yes, He went to the cross, but there was so much waiting for Him on the other side. Look at the Hebrews 12 verses on page 118 and write out all the good things that were on the other side of His suffering.

7. There are good things on the other side of your suffering as well. How does this help you endure what you're going through now?

> God was comforting this woman with the same comfort He'd given me. My heart was filled with joy. I felt a sense of redemption. And a renewed purpose rose up in me. My circumstances hadn't changed, but my certainty in God's plan being good had. I could see with my own eyes that none of my tears would be wasted. It wasn't the full picture—it didn't give me all the answers—but it was just enough to help me keep going. . . .
>
> I saw one woman being helped by my story. I saw one person's tears ease and hope rise. Yes, because I had dared to break my own secrecy, she could break hers. What a gift. . . .
>
> I made a difference, and what a difference that made in me. Wallowing in my suffering produces nothing but red eyes, bedhead, and a heart full of despair. But walking out the good things God purposes from my suffering produces eyes of hope, clearheaded thoughts, and a heart full of real joy.
>
> *It's Not Supposed to Be This Way*, pages 143–144

8. What is one thing you can do with your hardship or disappointment to make a difference in someone else's life? If necessary, keep this question with you until you find something and/or someone. Using your pain to make a difference will make an enormous difference for you and the person you're helping.

9. Read Romans 5:1–4. Do you recognize how your suffering is producing perseverance, as Paul promises in verse 4? What is one sign of perseverance you see in yourself?

DAYS 4&5: REVIEW AND READ

Catch-up time! Go back and complete any parts of the study and reflection from previous days this week that you weren't able to finish. Review any revelations you've had and reflect on any growth or personal insights you have gained. Make note of them here.

Spend the next two days reading chapters 9 and 10 in *It's Not Supposed to Be This Way*. Use the space below to note any insights or questions you want to bring to the next group session.

WEEK 5
SCHEDULE

BEFORE GROUP MEETING	Read Chapters 9–10 *It's Not Supposed to Be This Way* Book
GROUP MEETING	View Video Session 5: When the Enemy Comes Against Us Group Discussion Pages 124–134
PERSONAL STUDY DAY 1	Pages 135–140
PERSONAL STUDY DAY 2	Pages 140–143
PERSONAL STUDY DAY 3	Pages 144–145
PERSONAL STUDY DAY 4	Pages 145–147
DAY 5 BEFORE WEEK 6 GROUP MEETING	Read Chapter 11 *It's Not Supposed to Be This Way* Book Complete Any Unfinished Personal Study Activities

WHEN TH
ENEM
AGAIN

E

Y COMES

ST US

Session 5

WHEN THE ENEMY COMES AGAINST US

The enemy wants us to have an eroded trust in God and elevated trust in ourselves.

Welcome! (2 minutes)

Welcome to Session 5 of *It's Not Supposed to Be This Way*. A key part of getting to know God better is sharing your journey with others. Before watching the video, briefly share with one another any personal revelations you've had since the last session.

Opening Discussion (15 minutes)

Answer the following questions to prepare for this week's video teaching:

- What insights did you discover in your personal study from last week or in chapters 9–10 of *It's Not Supposed to Be This Way*?
- Share you answer to this question from last week's pesonal study: What would running forward with freedom look like for you?

VIDEO

When the Enemy Comes Against Us

(16:30 minutes)

LEADER:

Play the video segment for Session 5. Instruct your group to use the outline below to follow along or take additional notes on anything that stands out.

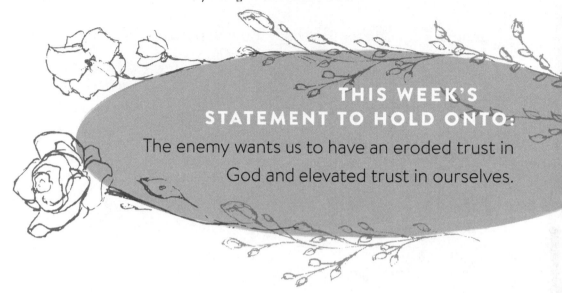

THIS WEEK'S STATEMENT TO HOLD ONTO: The enemy wants us to have an eroded trust in God and elevated trust in ourselves.

Shallow seeking will lead to shallow believing.

James 1:15: "Then, after desire has conceived, it gives birth to sin; and sin, when it is full-grown, gives birth to death."

Fears can either move us closer to God or draw us away.

1 John 2:15–17: the lust of the flesh, the lust of the eyes, and the pride of life

Genesis 3:6: good for food (lust of the flesh), pleasing to the eyes (lust of the eyes), and desirable for gaining wisdom (pride of life)

MATTHEW 4:1–11

v. 3: command these stones to become bread (lust of the flesh)

v. 9: all this I will give you if you bow down and worship me (lust of the eyes)

vv. 5–6: throw yourself down and he will command his angels concerning you (pride of life)

Look, linger, longing. We will steer where we stare.

God knows best. He can be trusted.

GROUP DISCUSSION

(45 minutes)

LEADER, READ EACH NUMBERED PROMPT TO THE GROUP.

1. What part of the teaching resonated with you the most?

2. Have someone read 1 John 2:15–17 aloud to the group:

   > [15]"Do not love the world or anything in the world. If anyone loves the world, love for the Father is not in them. [16]For everything in the world—the lust of the flesh, the lust of the eyes, and the pride of life—comes not from the Father but from the world. [17]The world and its desires pass away, but whoever does the will of God lives forever."

   - What does "the lust of the flesh" mean? How do you see it play out in everyday life?

   - What does "the lust of the eyes" mean? Give some examples of things we might lust for with our eyes.

   - What is "the pride of life"? How might we be driven by it?

3. When John says, "Do not love the world," he's referring to idolatry—the things we love and prioritize above God. Discuss some examples of how we might have misplaced desires and affections that pull us into idolatry.

4. Let's face our misplaced desires head-on. Finish the following sentences as if God is *not* part of the equation:

   I need _____.

   I desire _____.

   I deserve _____.

   Now complete the same sentences with God as your focus:

   I need _____.

   I desire _____.

   I deserve _____.

5. What did you learn about yourself from completing these sentences? How could the first set of statements make you vulnerable to temptation?

6. Often it's fear that leads us into temptation regarding our perceived needs, misplaced desires, and things we think we deserve:

   Lust of the flesh: "God's not going to provide what I need. I need to find comfort, pleasure, or relief my own way."

   Lust of the eyes: "God won't give me what I desire. I'm not satisfied with the things I have so I'm justified in getting more my own way."

   Pride of life: "God won't give me what I deserve. I'll pursue what makes me feel significant my own way."

- As a group, make a list of godly responses to each of the above three attitudes. Discuss how we can be intentional in times of temptation to remember the difference between our will and God's will.

LUST OF THE FLESH	LUST OF THE EYES	PRIDE OF LIFE

OPTIONAL GROUP ACTIVITY

(25 minutes)

If your group meets for two hours, include this activity as part of your meeting.

Satan lures us away from God's best by encouraging small desires that grow and give birth to sin that eventually give birth to death (James 1:13–15). In order to counter these desires before they take us a direction that will cause destruction, we need to remind ourselves daily of God's Truth.

1. What are the obstacles and distractions that prevent us from spending time in the Scriptures every day?

2. How can you overcome these obstacles and distractions?

3. Have someone read Matthew 4:1–11 aloud to the group. Underline the words "It is written" every time they appear.

   ¹Then Jesus was led by the Spirit into the wilderness to be tempted by the devil. ²After fasting forty days and forty nights, he was hungry. ³The tempter came to him and said, "If you are the Son of God, tell these stones to become bread."

   ⁴Jesus answered, "It is written: 'Man shall not live on bread alone, but on every word that comes from the mouth of God.'"

⁵Then the devil took him to the holy city and had him stand on the highest point of the temple. ⁶"If you are the Son of God," he said, "throw yourself down. For it is written:

> "'He will command his angels concerning you,
>> and they will lift you up in their hands,
>> so that you will not strike your foot against a stone.'"

⁷Jesus answered him, "It is also written: 'Do not put the Lord your God to the test.'"

⁸Again, the devil took him to a very high mountain and showed him all the kingdoms of the world and their splendor. ⁹"All this I will give you," he said, "if you will bow down and worship me."

¹⁰Jesus said to him, "Away from me, Satan! For it is written: 'Worship the Lord your God, and serve him only.'"

¹¹Then the devil left him, and angels came and attended him.

- Why do you think Satan quoted Scripture to Jesus (v. 6)? What do you learn about Satan from this?

- Jesus fought back against Satan's temptations by quoting Scripture. Every time He said, "It is written," He referred to verses from Deuteronomy chapters 6 and 8 in the Old Testament. Because He knew important passages of Scripture, He had them available in His mind when He needed them. What is a verse you could memorize that correlates to a temptation you're facing right now?

Please note: In chapter 10 of the book *It's Not Supposed to Be This Way* there are several pages of what Lysa calls "fighting words"—words to use when you need some help bringing your thoughts, emotions, and actions in line with what God says is true. This section of the book is a good place to start looking for Scripture to memorize. In your personal study this week, you'll take a couple of days to begin doing just that. The goal will be to think about what you've chosen to memorize so that Truth can sink deep into your heart and begin to influence the way you perceive life.

- Lysa described the process of temptation as one of *looking*, *lingering*, and *longing*. What is lingering? Why is it a problem? Give some examples where lingering can be a gateway to sin.

4. Turn in your Bible to James chapter 4. Have someone read verses 1–3 aloud to the group.

- According to James, what happens when we are left to our own desires?

5. Select another person to read verses 6–10 aloud to the group. This is James's antidote to the quarreling and coveting he talked about earlier.

- What do you think it means to submit yourself to God?

- How do we resist the devil when it comes to needs, desires, and what we think we deserve?

CLOSING ACTIVITY

What I Want to Remember (5 minutes)

Complete this activity on your own.

1. Briefly review the outline and any notes you took.

2. In the space below, write down the most significant thing you learned in this session—from the teaching, activities, or discussions.

WHAT I WANT TO
Remember
FROM THIS SESSION

Personal Prayer
(8 minutes)

Write a personal prayer here that reflects the area of this week's teaching you feel most in need of prayer.

CLOSING PRAYER

(2 minutes)

LEADER, READ THIS PRAYER ALOUD OVER THE GROUP BEFORE DISMASSAL:

Lord Jesus, we are surrounded and bombarded by temptations and subtle schemes of the enemy to pull us away from You. We have wrong beliefs about our needs, our desires, and what we deserve that are deeply ingrained in our hearts. We need Your help to reorient ourselves around what You say is true and what You want us to have. Lord, we know You are good and have our best interests in mind even when hard things are happening to us. Please help us walk in Your Truth. Please show us how we can help each other. We pray this in Your name, amen.

PERSONAL STUDY

DAY 1: REFLECT AND PRAY

Today you're going to reflect on chapter 9 of the book *It's Not Supposed to Be This Way*. If you haven't already read chapter 9, please do so now.

> It's heartbreaking to look into someone's eyes you deeply love and see sheer terror. She had made choices that slammed into her life like a wrecking ball. Her life no longer had soft edges and gentle places to land. Her choices had demolished what once was good into the sharp reality of a nightmare.
>
> I knew the enemy was doing what he does best: stealing, killing, destroying (John 10:10). When he sniffs out our interest in dangerous desires, he prowls around us with great intentionality. He doesn't know our thoughts, but he can certainly see when we start entertaining sinful possibilities and flirting with compromise.
>
> Her emotions were so deeply entangled with another man that she felt as if she would die without him. But at the same time the weight of guilt and shame was slowly squeezing the life out of her. She felt utterly destroyed, trapped, and miserable.
>
> *It's Not Supposed to Be This Way*, pages 152–153

1. What is your honest reaction to the story of Lysa's friend who got caught up in an affair? Do you feel fear, identification, judgment, compassion?

2. How does this story illustrate Lysa's teaching about disappointment leading to unmet desires that can leave us open to temptation? What were the disappointments that left Lysa's friend vulnerable?

3. "If the enemy can isolate us, he can influence us." What is one step you can take to make sure you're not leaving yourself vulnerable by being isolated?

> "You will begin to look at other people's lives and see all the shiny, new things they have. It will start off as a small seed of jealousy that will grow until you rationalize that you deserve those things too. You will make an extra purchase online and bend the monthly budget just a smidge. But it won't stop there. Sin and secrecy have ravenous appetites. Before you know it, you'll be hiding credit card bills from your husband, being dishonest in your relationships, and facing a growing amount of debt. Your seemingly small decisions today will not only affect you, but they'll ultimately lead to the division and possibly destruction of your family and the peace you took for granted."

It's Not Supposed to Be This Way, page 154

4. Above is the warning label that would go with the temptation to overspend. If your temptation had a warning label, what would it say?

5. Open your Bible and read James 1:21–22.

- What does "humbly accept the word planted in you" mean? Write down any area where you are currently vulnerable to not pay attention to God's Word.

> What my friend failed to realize was that she was being true to her most unhealthy self.
>
> If we are going to be true to ourselves, we'd better make sure we are being true to our most surrendered, healed, and healthy selves, the ones God made us to be. A great verse to help us determine this is Psalm 19:14:
>
> > May these words of my mouth and this meditation of my heart
> > be pleasing in your sight,
> > LORD, my Rock and my Redeemer.
>
> *It's Not Supposed to Be This Way*, page 165

6. If you were true to your most surrendered, healed, and healthy self, how would you deal with the desires that are currently most powerful in your life?

> Here's [Satan's] script:
> **Temptation:** Don't you want to feel good? Try this . . . it's amazing.
> **Deception:** You deserve this. You're special enough to get away with it. And no one will ever know. It will just be your well-deserved pleasure.
> **Accusation:** Look at what you've done now. God is ashamed of you.

When people find out, they will shame you and rename you as the loser you are. So you better keep it a secret. This isn't just a choice you made. This is who you really are. You'll never escape this shame or be healed of this pain. The best you can ever do is numb your pain, and I've got a few suggestions for how to do just that.

It's Not Supposed to Be This Way, pages 167–168

7. Counter each part of this script with words of truth from the Bible: Ephesians 2:1–5; Romans 8; James 4.

Temptation:

Deception:

Accusation:

The worst thing that can ever happen to Satan is for us to believe that God loves us, has our best in mind, and forgives us of our sin. Why does this strike fear in Satan's heart? Why does he want to keep you trapped in sin, wallowing in deception, and having to wade through the sinking sand of accusation? Because he wants you to keep your mouth shut. Isn't it interesting that we are told in Revelation 12:10 that Satan is the one who accuses us before God all day and all night? But the very next verse teaches us that the enemy is defeated by the blood of the Lamb and the word of our testimony.

Our enemy never wants a testimony to come from our lips. Therefore, he never wants us to experience freedom, truth, and redemption. Whether or not the dust of our lives is of our own making, he never wants it to get into the hands of God.

It's Not Supposed to Be This Way, page 166

8. How can you reject Satan's accusations and embrace God's redemption?

9. Read 1 Peter 1:6–7 below.

   [6]In all this you greatly rejoice, though now for a little while you may have had to suffer grief in all kinds of trials. [7]These have come so that the proven genuineness of your faith—of greater worth than gold, which perishes even though refined by fire—may result in praise, glory and honor when Jesus Christ is revealed.

   ● What can God do with your experience of temptation, deception, and accusation once you have surrendered these things to Him?

10. Read James 5:13–16 below.

   [13]Is anyone among you in trouble? Let them pray. Is anyone happy? Let them sing songs of praise. [14]Is anyone among you sick? Let them call the elders of the church to pray over them and anoint them with oil in the name of the Lord. [15]And the prayer offered in faith will make the sick person well; the Lord will raise them up. If they have sinned, they will be forgiven. [16]Therefore confess your sins to each other and pray for each other so that you may be healed. The prayer of a righteous person is powerful and effective.

- What does this passage urge you to do if you are struggling with temptation or have already fallen into sin?

DAY 2: STUDY AND REFLECT

Today you're going to reflect on chapter 10 of the book *It's Not Supposed to Be This Way.* If you haven't already read chapter 10, please do so now.

1. In John 16:33 below, what is the significance of the words "in me"?

   "I have told you these things, so that in me you may have peace. In this world you will have trouble. But take heart! I have overcome the world."

2. Read 1 Peter 4:12–13 below.

   [12]Dear friends, do not be surprised at the fiery ordeal that has come on you to test you, as though something strange were happening to you. [13]But rejoice inasmuch as you participate in the sufferings of Christ, so that you may be overjoyed when his glory is revealed.

   - What does it mean to participate in Christ's sufferings? How are you doing that?

3. Lysa writes, "But comfort isn't a solution to seek; rather, it's a by-product we'll reap when we stay close to the Lord." How is that relevant to the situation you're currently facing and the solution you're currently seeking?

What if the comfort and certainties we crave today are a deadly recipe for complacency that will draw our hearts further and further away from God? There are many examples of this in the Bible, but let's look at one tucked into Jeremiah:

> Moab has been at rest from youth, like wine left on its dregs, not poured from one jar to another—she has not gone into exile. So she tastes as she did, and her aroma is unchanged. (Jeremiah 48:11)

It's Not Supposed to Be This Way, page 181

4. What is "complacency"? How does Jeremiah 48:11 illustrate it?

5. Describe how complacency sometimes affects your spiritual life.

6. Why do you think God views complacency as a greater danger to our relationship with Him than suffering?

Just as we have to get off the couch and pour ourselves into working out if we want to gain physical strength, we have to be poured into circumstances that will result in our being transformed if we want to gain spiritual strength. In the middle of our disappointments and hard times, we must seek to be transformed into thinking biblically, processing with truth instinctively, and trusting God implicitly.

We must get rid of the dregs—weakness, fear, complacency, and the hopeless resignation that all of life is unfair and God is unjust. To sit in those dregs will cause us to absorb more and more of the world's way of thinking. To think like the world leads to death—death of hope, death of peace, death of joy. But to think like Christ is to have fresh life breathed inside of us and His peace radiating from us.

It's Not Supposed to Be This Way, page 183

7. Have you ever experienced "the hopeless resignation that all of life is unfair and God is unjust"? What is the biblical response to that resignation?

8. What does it mean to think biblically, and how are you doing this currently?

If we want to know God's will, God's perspective, God's good that He has in store for us, then we must not be conformed to the world's way of processing life but be transformed by God's Word and God's way: "Do not conform to the pattern of this world, but be transformed by the renewing of your mind. Then you will be able to test and approve what God's will is—his good, pleasing and perfect will" (Romans 12:2).

It's Not Supposed to Be This Way, page 184

9. Describe the world's way of processing the disappointments you are currently dealing with.

10. What is the biblical response? For your answer, read Isaiah 43:1–5a (AMP) and write what you learn below.

> ¹But now, this is what the LORD, your Creator says, O Jacob,
>   And He who formed you, O Israel,
> "Do not fear, for I have redeemed you [from captivity];
>   I have called you by name; you are Mine!
> ²"When you pass through the waters, I will be with you;
>   And through the rivers, they will not overwhelm you.
> When you walk through fire, you will not be scorched,
>   Nor will the flame burn you.
> ³"For I am the LORD your God,
>   The Holy One of Israel, your Savior;
> I have given Egypt [to the Babylonians] as your ransom,
>   Cush (ancient Ethiopia) and Seba [its province] in exchange for you.
> ⁴"Because you are precious in My sight,
>   You are honored and I love you,
> I will give *other* men in return for you
>   and *other* peoples in exchange for your life.
> ⁵"Do not fear, for I am with you. . . ."

DAY 3: STUDY AND REFLECT

1. The fighting words at the end of chapter 10 are worth some time and attention. Go to pages 191–202 of *It's Not Supposed to Be This Way* and review the declarations and Scripture passages that help with each area of our lives:

   > Affection—my heart, what I love
   > Adoration—my mouth, what I worship
   > Attention—my mind, what I focus on
   > Attraction—my eyes, what I desire
   > Ambition—my calling, what I spend my time seeking
   > Action—my choices, how I stand firm

   Which declaration and Scripture passage spoke to your heart and circumstances the most? Write that verse here:

2. Why did you choose that one? How does it intersect with your current circumstances?

3. Today you're going to make this declaration your own. Start by reading it aloud. Then choose two sentences from the declaration and one sentence from the Scripture passage and write them here. Choose sentences that you especially need to impress upon your heart and have available to you when you need them.

   Take 10 minutes to really think on and pray over these sentences.

4. Type the words from the declaration, along with your Scripture excerpt, into a note on your phone. Put a checkmark here when you've completed this. ☐

By doing this, you can keep these words with you during the day and come back to them whenever you have a free moment. Commit to yourself that when you have a few minutes to check your phone, you will check your declaration first and read it through, preferably aloud, before checking other things.

DAY 4: STUDY AND REFLECT

Before you do your final reading tomorrow, take some time today to reflect back on all you've learned in this study so far.

Look back through this study guide and focus especially on what you wrote in each session for "What I Want to Remember." The five statements to hold onto are included below as reminders of each session topic.

- What would happen in our lives if we really lived in the absolute assurance of God's love in the midst of our disappointments?
- Jesus learned through His suffering an obedience that matured over time.
- God's promise fulfilled applies both to problems placed on us and problems within us.
- Turn the tragedy of sin into a victorious testimony.
- The enemy wants us to have an eroded trust in God and elevated trust in ourselves.

What are the key things you learned from each session of this study?

SESSION 1

SESSION 2

SESSION 3

SESSION 4

SESSION 5

What was the most important thing you learned about yourself?

How did you experience God's presence or grace?

What was the most important thing you learned about God?

Is there a friend you could encourage with these insights? Invite that friend to coffee, write them a letter, or just call them to talk.

If your group decides to do the optional discussion at next week's meeting, you'll have the opportunity to talk about your answers as well as look at some other reflection questions.

DAY 5: REVIEW AND READ

Catch-up time! Go back and complete any parts of the study and reflection from previous days this week that you weren't able to finish. Review any revelations you've had and reflect on any growth or personal insights you have gained. Make note of them here.

Spend today reading the final chapter in *It's Not Supposed to Be This Way*, chapter 11. Use the space below to note any insights or questions you want to bring to the next group session.

WEEK 6
SCHEDULE

BEFORE GROUP MEETING	Read Chapter 11 *It's Not Supposed to Be This Way* Book
FINAL GROUP MEETING	View Video Session 6: Kingdom Minded, Eternally Focused Group Discussion Pages 152–164
PERSONAL STUDY WRAP-UP	Pages 165–169

KINGDOM
ETERN
FOCUSE

MINDED

ALLY

D

Session 6

KINGDOM MINDED, ETERNALLY FOCUSED

How we live on this side of eternity matters.

Welcome! (2 minutes)

Welcome to Session 6 of *It's Not Supposed to Be This Way*. A key part of getting to know God better is sharing your journey with others. Before watching the video, briefly share with one another any personal revelations you've had since the last session.

Opening Discussion (15 minutes)

Answer the following questions to prepare for this week's video teaching:

- How are you thinking differently about temptation?
- Which one of the fighting words did you choose to focus on?

VIDEO

Kingdom Minded, Eternally Focused (21 minutes)

LEADER:

Play the video segment for Session 6. Instruct your group to use the outline below to follow along or take additional notes on anything that stands out.

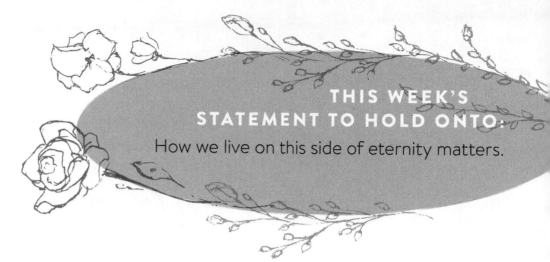

THIS WEEK'S STATEMENT TO HOLD ONTO:

How we live on this side of eternity matters.

Kingdom minded means there's a purpose to my pain here and now.

PHILIPPIANS 4:5–7

The Lord is near. In every situation present your requests to God.

JAMES 1:2–4

Consider it pure joy. The testing of your faith produces perseverance.

Eternally focused: We are heading to a restored Eden.

JAMES 1:12

The crown of life is for those who suffer for the sake of the gospel.

1 PETER 5:2–4

The crown of glory is for those who fulfill the role of elder or pastor.

1 THESSALONIANS 2:19–20; PHILIPPIANS 4:1

The crown of rejoicing is for those who win others to Christ.

2 TIMOTHY 4:8

The crown of righteousness is for anyone who perseveres through hardship and longs for the return of Jesus.

1 CORINTHIANS 9:25–27

The *incorruptible crown* is for those who keep their body in a whole and healthy state on mission for God.

We will cast our crowns at Jesus' feet.

GROUP DISCUSSION

(45 minutes)

LEADER, READ EACH NUMBERED PROMPT TO THE GROUP.

1. What part of the teaching had the most profound impact on you?

2. "Kingdom minded" means there's a purpose to your pain here and now that has implications for God's kingdom. We've looked at James 1:2–4 before, but let's examine it again now.

    > ²Consider it pure joy, my brothers and sisters, whenever you face trials of many kinds, ³because you know that the testing of your faith produces perseverance. ⁴Let perseverance finish its work so that you may be mature and complete, not lacking anything.

    - Why is perseverance necessary for maturity? Why is it important for you to become mature and complete?

    - Lysa explained "mature and complete, not lacking anything" by describing a cake, that requires even those ingredients we might want to leave out if we were to taste them raw. How might your disappointments and sufferings be part of the process to make you mature and complete?

- James doesn't say "feel the joy" but instead "consider it pure joy." In other words, "consider where some glimpses of joy might be even in the midst of all the hurt." How is that a helpful distinction for you?

3. Remember, Jesus understands our hurt and pain. He is our empathetic high priest. He can be sensitive to us in our need because of His experience of suffering on earth and on the cross. But Jesus' suffering was also for our greater good. Another possible purpose to your pain is to equip you to comfort others:

> [3]Praise be to the God and Father of our Lord Jesus Christ, the Father of compassion and the God of all comfort, [4]who comforts us in all our troubles, so that we can comfort those in any trouble with the comfort we ourselves receive from God. (2 Corinthians 1:3–4)

- Why do you think it's comforting to others when they know we have suffered or are suffering in the same way?

- What comfort have you received from God, either directly or through other people?

- Have you had any opportunities to comfort others with the comfort you have received?

These are just two of the many possible purposes of a person's pain. You may never know the answer to "Why?" in this lifetime. Or it may take years before you get a glimpse of why.

4. In the midst of it all on this side of eternity, we can remember the truth found in Psalm 34:18, "The LORD is close to the brokenhearted and saves those who are crushed in spirit." How have you experienced this?

"Eternally focused" means we are headed to a restored Eden. The apostle Paul had his eyes firmly fixed on eternity. He wrote about his own sufferings to the Corinthians and said,

> [8]We are hard pressed on every side, but not crushed; perplexed, but not in despair; [9]persecuted, but not abandoned; struck down, but not destroyed. [10]We always carry around in our body the death of Jesus, so that the life of Jesus may also be revealed in our body. (2 Corinthians 4:8–10)

5. How do you think it was possible for Paul to be hard pressed but not crushed?

6. How does this give you courage in your own journey?

Look at the contrasts Paul points out in verses 8–10:

the dying of Jesus	the life of Jesus
hard pressed	but not crushed
perplexed	but not in despair
persecuted	but not abandoned
struck down	but not destroyed[3]

7. How can you relate to some of the words used to describe the dying of Jesus?

8. What do you think it means to have the life of Jesus revealed in you here and now, even in the midst of your struggles?

Paul then goes on to say that the reason why he keeps speaking about Jesus is that he knows that one day the Father, who raised Jesus from the dead, will also raise us:

> [13]It is written: "I believed; therefore I have spoken." Since we have that same spirit of faith, we also believe and therefore speak, [14]because we know that the one who raised the Lord Jesus from the dead will also raise us with Jesus and present us with you to himself. [15]All this is for your benefit, so that the grace that is reaching more and more people may cause thanksgiving to overflow to the glory of God. (2 Corinthians 4:13–15)

9. Where does Paul's spiritual confidence come from?

10. Paul says that "the grace that is reaching more and more people" (because of his ministry) is causing "thanksgiving to overflow to the glory of God." Have you ever considered creating this same type of thanksgiving because you told people what you've been through and they can see what God is doing in you?

Finally Paul says,

> [16]Therefore we do not lose heart. Though outwardly we are wasting away, yet inwardly we are being renewed day by day. [17]For our light and momentary troubles are achieving for us an eternal glory that far outweighs them all. [18]So we fix our eyes not on what is seen, but on what is unseen, since what is seen is temporary, but what is unseen is eternal. (2 Corinthians 4:16–18)

11. What are the temporary, seen things in your life?

12. What are the unseen and eternal things that far outweigh what is temporary and seen?

In Session 2 you looked at those unseen and eternal things as described in Revelation 21–22. Today let's consider a passage from Isaiah that describes them. Have someone read aloud:

> ⁶On this mountain the Lord Almighty will prepare
>   a feast of rich food for all peoples,
> a banquet of aged wine—
>   the best of meats and the finest of wines.
> ⁷On this mountain he will destroy
>   the shroud that enfolds all peoples,
> the sheet that covers all nations;
>   ⁸he will swallow up death forever.
> The Sovereign Lord will wipe away the tears
>   from all faces;
> he will remove his people's disgrace
>   from all the earth.
> The Lord has spoken.
> ⁹In that day they will say,
> "Surely this is our God;
>   we trusted in him, and he saved us.
> This is the Lord, we trusted in him;
>   let us rejoice and be glad in his salvation." (Isaiah 25:6–9)

13. How does Isaiah describe the restored Eden? What overlaps with what you read in Revelation? What is new?

14. What can we learn about our destiny from thinking of it as a feast? What does feasting mean to you?

15. How does thinking about the restored Eden ahead of you help you deal with disappointments now?

16. How does it affect you to think about the crowns that you will be able to place at the feet of Jesus?

OPTIONAL GROUP ACTIVITY

Review (25 minutes)

If your group meets for two hours, allow 20 minutes for this discussion.

1. Refer back to the questions you answered on Day 4 of the Session 5 study. Discuss these as a group now.

2. How has this study affected you—for example, in your attitudes, behaviors, or relationships?

3. C. S. Lewis writes:

> Indeed, if we consider the unblushing promises of reward and the staggering nature of the rewards promised in the Gospels, it would seem that Our Lord finds our

desires not too strong, but too weak. We are half-hearted creatures, fooling about with drink and sex and ambition when infinite joy is offered us, like an ignorant child who wants to go on making mud pies in a slum because he cannot imagine what is meant by the offer of a holiday at the sea. We are far too easily pleased.[4]

How does this quote speak to you in light of all that we've studied this week?

4. How has God helped you become more kingdom minded and eternally focused?

5. Is there a passage of Scripture that has been especially important to you in this study? What is it?

6. How are you dealing with your disappointment or pain differently now than at the beginning of the study?

CLOSING ACTIVITY

What I Want to Remember (5 minutes)

Complete this activity on your own.

1. Briefly review the outline and any notes you took.

2. In the space below, write down the most significant thing you learned in this session—from the teaching, activities, or discussions.

Personal Prayer
(8 minutes)

Write a personal prayer here that reflects the area of this week's teaching you feel most in need in prayer. Include any praises for breakthroughs you may have experienced during the overall study.

CLOSING PRAYER

(2 minutes)

**LEADER, READ THIS PRAYER ALOUD OVER
THE GROUP BEFORE DISMISSAL:**

Thank You, Lord, for giving us these Truths—these insights, these life-giving perspectives to hold onto as we process everything we walk through. Make us more joyful, peaceful, and faithful people. Help us build our lives around a confidence in Your goodness and a secure hope for all that lies ahead of us now and into eternity. Thank You for helping us, healing us, holding us, and making us stronger and more beautiful than ever before. We boldly declare today that we trust You and we love You. Amen.

PERSONAL STUDY

STUDY AND REFLECT

Today you're going to reflect on chapter 11 of the book *It's Not Supposed to Be This Way*. If you haven't already read chapter 11, please do so now.

> Dust is messy.
>
> We don't even like to touch dust, especially if it's made up of the shattered pieces of our own hearts.
>
> Thankfully, we don't have to. We can hand it over to God—the One who forms our dust into something we want but never could have made for ourselves.
>
> *It's Not Supposed to Be This Way*, pages 208–209

1. How have you seen God form something out of the dust in your life?

2. In what ways can you continue to entrust this process of healing and restoration to the Lord?

To live is to love. To love is to risk pain. To risk pain is to live. It's what it means to truly be human. As fragile as dust. The breaking of us. The making of us. The building up of our faith.

Tears are the truest connection we have with others, and trust is the truest connection we have with God. Angie's tears of gratitude touched a deep part of me and helped me to think with a heart of gratitude and trust as I wrestled with my own tears.

And doesn't it all come down to that? Trust. Trading our will for "Thy will," because we know He will.

It's Not Supposed to Be This Way, pages 211–212

3. "To live is to love. To love is to risk pain. To risk pain is to live." Understanding that all humans are fragile, how can you love others with more grace?

4. How can you have a marked moment of trading your will for God's will?

Then I'd hold up my written rules for paintbrush holders and clear my throat in a dramatic fashion.

- Everyone must try.
- Give yourself permission not to be perfect.
- Refuse to be intimidated by the process.
- The most beauty will emerge from the paintbrushes held by those who are most free from fear.

- Smile. I already love what will soon come to life on your canvas.

We'd relax and realize these are also good rules for life.

It's Not Supposed to Be This Way, pages 215–216

5. Even though these are the guidelines Lysa uses for painting, they're really about vulnerability. Which of these challenges you the most?

6. Which one of these are you currently demonstrating?

"As she seeks Me in her mess, she will show others how to find freedom from that weight. She will be a force to be reckoned with in the great battle of good versus evil. Her gentleness will be her strength. Her love will be the fiercest weapon. Her balance will be the beauty of her soul. And her wrestling with the answers to why? that never come will be her humility.

"She'll be a learner and a lover of truth. She will crave certainty. But people are unpredictable, and circumstances will often cause her confusion. So, she'll take her uncertainties and bury them in the rich soil of My Word.

"These will be some of our closest times together, she and I. When she learns something while confused—she'll remember it forever. Truth will shape her in the best of ways and lead her heart to want to give the hope she's found to others. So it's through her uncertainties she'll find her most certain purpose in the world."

It's Not Supposed to Be This Way, pages 218–219

7. The above passage comes from the allegorical dialogue between the Father and the Son called "Upside Down" on pages 217–222 of the book. Take a moment to imagine these words being true of you. Then choose one of these sentences and write why this is so meaningful to you personally.

8. Lysa wrote out a prayer of restoration that she could pray over her life and her disappointments. (You can read her prayer by going to https://proverbs31.org/gifts-for-you.) Write out your own prayer of restoration using the space provided on the next page, declaring the good things God has done to renew and restore your heart in this study.